SACRED
RESISTANCE

Praise for *Sacred Resistance*

"Ginger Gaines-Cirelli does us all a favor here by redefining *resistance*, taking it out of the temporal realm of today's politics and moving it to a place where committed Christians can determine to fight injustice and live lives of hope and love for God and community."
—Mike McCurry, former White House Press Secretary; director and professor, Center for Public Theology, Wesley Theological Seminary, Washington, DC

"Ginger Gaines-Cirelli combines the heart of a pastor, the wisdom of a biblical theologian, the spiritual discipline of a Christian contemplative, and the passion of a prophet with genuine humility and joy to offer a word that will inspire, challenge, and equip faithful disciples to be more faithful witnesses for Christ. This book is deeply rooted in scripture interpreted through reason, experience, and tradition and emerges out of the life of a pastor serving a vibrant congregation in the heart of the nation's capital. It is the word we need 'for such a time as this.'"
—James Harnish, United Methodist pastor, retired; author of *Make a Difference: Following Your Passion and Finding Your Place to Serve*; *A Disciple's Heart: Growing in Love and Grace*; and other books from Abingdon Press

"Christians on both the right and left of the American political divide often bring their politics into their churches rather than forming their political views in light of their faith. Ginger Gaines-Cirelli reminds us that faithful public witness is grounded not in our passionate views about the latest hot-button issue but rather in a vision of God's wholeness. Sacred resistance is a theological posture and a spiritual worldview shaped by the prophetic imagination, the cross of Christ, and the heart of God."
—Ann A. Michel, Associate Director of the Lewis Center for Church Leadership, Wesley Theological Seminary, Washington, DC

SACRED RESISTANCE

A Practical Guide
to Christian Witness and Dissent

Ginger Gaines-Cirelli

Abingdon Press
Nashville

SACRED RESISTANCE:
A PRACTICAL GUIDE TO CHRISTIAN WITNESS AND DISSENT

Copyright © 2018 by Abingdon Press

This book is printed on acid-free paper.

Library of Congress Cataloging-in-Publication Data has been requested.

ISBN 978-1-5018-5685-3

All scripture quotations, unless otherwise noted, are taken from the New Revised Standard Version of the Bible, copyright 1989, Division of Christian Education of the National Council of the Churches of Christ in the United States of America. Used by permission. All rights reserved.

Scripture quotations marked (NIV) are taken from the Holy Bible, New International Version®, NIV®. Copyright © 1973, 1978, 1984, 2011 by Biblica, Inc.™ Used by permission of Zondervan. All rights reserved worldwide. www.zondervan.com. The "NIV" and "New International Version" are trademarks registered in the United States Patent and Trademark Office by Biblica, Inc.™

Hafiz's poem "A Great Need" is from *THE GIFT* by Daniel Ladinsky, copyright 1999, used with permission.

The poem "Peace" is by Skye Green, a 2013 graduate of St. Augustine Academy in Bridgeport, Connecticut. Used by permission. All rights reserved.

The poems "1991: I" and "2008: I" are from *This Day* by Wendell Berry. Copyright © 2013 by Wendell Berry. Reprinted by permission of Counterpoint Press.

18 19 20 21 22 23 24 25 26 27—10 9 8 7 6 5 4 3 2 1
MANUFACTURED IN THE UNITED STATES OF AMERICA

For T. C.
whose faithful witness embodies sacred resistance

CONTENTS

PREFACE

*Resistance is the protest of those who hope, and hope
is the feast of the people who resist.*

—Jürgen Moltmann

The election results were in and Sunday was coming. Never in my life had I felt the kind of weight and responsibility that pressed in on me over the course of those four days. Not only in my city of Washington, DC, but also across the nation, many people from across the political spectrum were stunned at the outcome of the 2016 presidential election. Whether from a place of elation or despair, everyone scrambled to make sense of what was happening, what the results meant, and how to deal with the range of emotions that erupted in private and public. Journalists and bloggers furiously spun linguistic tapestries of polling data and political theory, social commentary, and even strident blame. I immersed myself in the Strum and Drang, hoping to discern some glimpse of God's beckoning. The scripture I planned to preach, Luke 21:5-19, the foretelling of the temple's destruction, was another primary source in my discernment over those days. Sunday was coming and I knew that the congregation I serve [located within a mile of the White House] would come hungry for a nourishing word.

But what was the word that would truly nourish? My personal challenge in those four days was to allow myself to attend to my own personal feelings while keeping perspective of the larger picture. I struggled to resist being pulled into polarized, absolutized scapegoating and blaming scenarios, on the one hand, and capitulation to any easy "peace," on the other. Energies pulled at me to preach reconciliation, patience, and forbearance while other energies pushed me toward rage and revolution. Was it possible to stand in the midst of it all in a way that had at least the potential to offer "food that satisfies?" (Isa 55). One thing I knew for certain was that there was no way one person could speak a nourishing word into *all* that would walk through the door that Sunday. Some would leave hungry, and some might even feel poisoned.

There came a moment in prayer when two things emerged with clarity. The first was that I had to tell the truth as I perceived it. The second was that, together with the congregation I serve, I choose to stand with the poor, the vulnerable, and the oppressed. If I was going to err, it would be by risking too much for those two convictions. After proclaiming that in so many words at the beginning of the sermon, I also said:

Today, this gathered body and our nation as a whole is facing trials and temptations. There is suffering and struggle, division and demonization, anger and confusion, fear and deep uncertainty. I hear blame flowing in every possible direction. Theories about what is going on in our nation abound. The "problem" is described in terms of rural versus urban, white versus black, educated versus undereducated, establishment versus antiestablishment, rich versus poor. "Versus" is the only common denominator.... The "problem," depending upon who is speaking, is "coastal elites" or immigrants or evangelicals or Muslims or the media. The best I can tell, there is not just one "problem" but rather a whole mess of deep-seated and often interrelated issues that have contributed to our current situation. In this and every moment of deep division and struggle, subtlety and nuance and the realities of history and complex intersections in human community are often lost as we cast about for some scapegoat for our own anxiety and fear and rage. But there is no quick "fix." Blaming someone won't bring transformation.

This is not to say that there is nothing to be called out, renounced, and challenged. Lord knows Jesus didn't mince words with purveyors of injustice. But Jesus never ever acted with violence or hatred or deceit. He was angry at the death-dealing ways of empire; he was angry at the perversion of religious law. But Jesus's anger was fueled by his love for people and a desire for all people to experience the liberating love of God and life in God's Kin-dom; it was not an anger seeking a scapegoat, but rather reconciliation, mercy, and justice.

You and I find ourselves in this complicated and volatile moment in our nation's history, gathered as a community who bear the name of Jesus the Christ. And Jesus speaks to us today saying: "This will give you an opportunity to testify" (Luke 21:13). What will your testimony be? How are you going to respond? How are you going to choose to live?[1]

It was in this context and in response to those questions that the language and ministry of "sacred resistance" emerged in my heart, mind, and congregation.

To be clear, this work is not new. The struggle for justice and resistance to that which is counter to God's Kin-dom[2] has been around forever. One can argue (as I will do later in this book) that God's prophets have been at this work from the very moment they stepped onto the scene. Mobilization of people of faith for racial justice, economic justice, environmental justice, gender justice, and LGBTQ justice is a rich and deeply powerful ongoing reality in the United States. But in this historical moment, it seems we are witnessing a kind of awakening. The deep brokenness of the present moment is prompting many to wake up who, through privilege or complacency, were willfully ignorant of the suffering of so many across our nation or, if not ignorant, at least unmotivated to do anything about it. The bold-faced prejudice, racism, bullying, and nastiness on display in the public square appear to have shaken many out of our privileged slumber. There is evidence of a growing desire and willingness to mine the depths of our faith for resources to fuel and guide solidarity with siblings who are the targets of injustice, violence, and hatred. For those who have been living with those targets on their backs forever, this latest surge of concern may feel anemic or wretchedly late. Justice is overdue. That is as true now as it was when, from a jail cell in Birmingham, Alabama, in 1963, the Rev. Dr. Martin Luther King Jr. wrote of "legitimate and unavoidable impatience" with the realities of racism and the pace of any substantive change.

But if something has pricked the conscience of many in our nation in a way that motivates greater solidarity with those whose backs are against the wall, we would be foolish not to do all we can to provide support.

I say this humbly and with gratitude for those who have come alongside to convict and guide me over the years as I have awakened to the realities of suffering and injustice in our world. My "waking up" has been more sluggish than I care to admit, and I come to this present work even as I struggle to continue removing the scales of privilege from my eyes. As a white, cisgender, financially secure, able-bodied, English-speaking, highly educated female United States citizen who is married to a man, there are a lot of scales to remove! It is a journey both humbling and strengthening and I have "miles to go before I sleep." While I seek to be mindful of language and assumptions and want only to speak in ways that are "useful for building up" (Eph 4:29), I am sure that in the course of these pages, I will stumble and speak in a way that does harm. For that, I can only acknowledge my limit and the expectation that, through the writing and response to this project, I will have the opportunity to confront new "blind spots."

What I bring to this work is a love of God, a love for people, a passion for creating loving and just community, and a deep impatience with "all that kills abundant living."[3] I believe that theology matters, not just as fancy decoration for our primarily activist or pastoral rooms, but as the very foundation and framework for the Christian life in all its manifestations. And I bring a "hunger and thirst for righteousness"; I'm convinced that same hunger and thirst is shared by people everywhere though expressed in myriad ways. Finally, I am a person of deep hope. I resist because my hope is in God. And, thanks be to God, my resistance draws me near to evidences that hope is not in vain.

ACKNOWLEDGMENTS

Foundry United Methodist Church in Washington, DC, is the context in which this project was both conceived and brought to fruition. Foundry's historic witness and continued commitment to live and lead in prophetic ways inspire these words and push me to live my faith more deeply and courageously. Without the support of the congregation, clergy, and staff of Foundry over the past year, this book would not exist. I am deeply grateful. I particularly want to thank Rev. Dawn Hand for managing the wondrous and challenging day-to-day life of Foundry during my long writing retreats, and Rev. Ben Roberts and the members of the Sacred Resistance Ministry Team at Foundry who have taken up this work with faithfulness and skill. In particular, Tracy Content, Andrew Lee, Jennifer Parsons, and Meera Fickling have made key contributions.

In the process of writing, I have been aware of the influences of all the congregations I have been privileged to serve. Each embodies sacred resistance in its own way and has guided my heart and mind in the ways of creating cross-shaped community. At this stage of my ministry, there are too many congregations to list, but you know who you are. You have blessed and taught me.

The team at The United Methodist Publishing House—Paul Franklyn, Sonua Bohannon, Peggy Shearon, the whole production team, and especially my editor Constance Stella—have been encouraging, supportive, and patient throughout this process. I'm not certain who initially spotted my social media hashtag (#sacredresistance), but someone at the publishing house was the instigator of this project! I appreciate the opportunity and the nudge to step up to this work.

Committed disciples from the Foundry congregation have worked since 2016 to develop the church's Sacred Resistance Ministry. I am grateful to them and to Rev. Ben Roberts for taking up this work with faithfulness and skill. Team members including Tracy Content, Andrew Lee, Jennifer Parsons, and Meera Fickling have produced an extremely helpful document, which can be found online at **sacredresistance.net**. It includes their mission statement along with a description of how they got started, the ministry's logistics, and an honest assessment of the challenges they've faced. They describe their hopes and plans for this still-evolving ministry. And they've included an extraordinarily useful list of things for similar groups and congregations to keep in mind. If you are interested in beginning a sacred resistance ministry of any kind, I urge you to visit **sacredresistance.net** and read this brief resource.

Many colleagues have provided concrete examples of Sacred Resistance as it takes shape in community. Their stories are shared as supplemental material that can also be found at **www.sacredresistance.net**. Many thanks to Hal Garman and the Gaithersburg Beloved Community Initiative; Melissa Maher and the people of Mercy Street in Houston; Rachel Baughman and the people of Oak Lawn UMC in Dallas and Safe Spaces Lebanon; the people of First UMC in Birmingham, Alabama; Helen Ryde, Brook van der Linde, and the people of Haywood Street Congregation in Asheville, North Carolina; Amanda Garber and the people of RISE in Harrisonburg, Virginia; Kaji Dousa and Park Avenue Christian Church in NYC; Rebecca Voelkel and the Center for Sustainable Justice in Minneapolis–St. Paul; and Guthrie Graves-Fitzsimmons and his project *The Resistance Prays*.

All of us need companions on the journey of faith and struggle. Mine include the folks in "Sunday Salon," my clergywomen's covenant group, my "first Friday" dinner dates, and clergy colleagues from across my life of ministry. But the companion I depend upon most is my spouse, Anthony, who for more than twenty years has helped me learn what love and courage look like. To him I am indebted most of all.

INTRODUCTION

"Resistance"

The language of "resistance" has a long history. Most folks living today might associate it with the movement in the Second World War involving espionage, sabotage, and even guerrilla attacks against the Nazi regime. It's been embodied by those who've marched, stood on picket lines, participated in sit-ins, and put their bodies between trucks, tanks, and other people or cherished land. Eminent political theorist Michael Walzer defines resistance as "a defensive politics...a form of collective civil disobedience. It involves physical presence and solidarity; it appeals to moral law or human rights; it is usually illegal but non-violent; it is locally and communally based; its activists are angry citizens and lower-level officials."[1]

In that same essay, Walzer makes a distinction between actions like a sit-in or nonpayment of taxes and the larger movement or issue those actions seek to address. For him, *resistance* is the word describing the actions but not the larger issue. He contends that resistance is only "half a politics." It is important and absolutely necessary but tends to be spontaneous, short-lived, defensive, and limited.[2]

I understand and support Walzer's definition of "resistance" used as a political term. Short-term acts of local "resistance" (defensive action) need to be matched by broad-based political movements (offensive action) that include "organization, strategic thinking, and tactical discipline." However, I am not a political theorist or activist; I am a pastor-theologian and a follower of Jesus. The language of "resistance" has evolved in my prayer, thinking, and practice in a slightly different way. But before I get into that, it is important to address the issue of politics in church.

A Word on "Politics"

Over the years, I have served congregations in which the generally accepted perspective was that "politics don't belong in church." While I support the desire to create a space guarded against the rancor and bruising speech of partisan politics, I believe that wherever the Bible is read, "politics," in its true sense, is present. The word *politics* derives from the Greek word *polis*, which means "city" or "body of citizens" and therefore has to do with the ways humans live in community. The biblical story is the story of a God who from the very beginning is focused on the world and pays attention to the ways humans live in community, who cares about what we do and how we do it, who desires that we live in love, mutuality, and reverence for creation and for the dignity of all human life.

Throughout history God engages in the political world, sending prophets, teachers of wisdom, and witnesses of the way to remind us of who we are, of what is possible, and of God's presence and power. Moses is sent to liberate a people enslaved by the Egyptian empire. Esther risks her life by breaking the royal law in order to save her people from holocaust. The people Israel are called to be "a light to the nations" (Isa 42:6). When Israel grows forgetful and turns away, prophet after prophet come to call the people away from the idolatry of self-made gods and military superpowers and toward YHWH. God's messengers call us to embody the ways of justice, mercy, humility, and peace—for the sake of *life* ("Listen, so that you may live" [Isa 55:3b]).

Jesus, the fulfillment of the prophetic tradition, came into the world "that they may have *life*" (John 10:10). Jesus says his "job description" is to proclaim good news to the poor, release to the captives, recovery to the infirm, and liberation to the oppressed (Luke 4:18-19). To be a disciple of Jesus is to acknowledge we follow one whose focus is *the world* and its people—especially its suffering people. Jesus doesn't focus on the poor and suffering because of a limited love, but because of an expansive love that desires all people to live in truly human dignity—a dignity befitting children of God. As long as there are oppressor and oppressed, then life is not lived in its fullness for anyone.

As Christians, we know that Jesus's crime was calling out the oppressors even as he cared for the oppressed. Jesus's insistence on hearing and seeing the ignored; lifting up the lowly; knocking the powerful down a few notches; touching the untouchable; caring for children; encountering all people with equal dignity; healing the sick in body, mind, and spirit; challenging the hardened interpretations of religious law; and trusting God more than human idols of wealth, privilege, or honor placed him on the "public enemy" lists of the political elite. As a result, Jesus became an innocent victim of injustice who was crucified by the power players and policies of the religious establishment and the state.

In all this, it is clear that God's concern and engagement in human lives, community, and relationship is not confined only to our interpersonal lives or little religious enclaves. God is also engaged and engaging in the *polis*, in the everyday, messy, lived reality of the world and its people. Whether we like it or not, we are called to engage there, too.

"Sacred" Resistance

Since Christians follow one who is not only willing but also determined to help us work our stuff out in community and to live together with love and justice, resistance to hatred and injustice seems an obvious expression of our faith. But what, if anything, makes our resistance different from anyone else's? What makes resistance "sacred"?

It is not merely that Christian people join in public political actions while wearing their religious T-shirts. It is not merely that Christian people host press conferences, rallies, or organizational meetings for social justice causes at their religious buildings. It is not merely that clergy preach against the "isms" in their sermons or speak of peace in their public prayers. These activities are important and provide a powerful public witness to sacred resistance, but they do not constitute its reality.

Over the past year, I have repeatedly said that "sacred resistance is a movement not a moment." While those words are certainly a rallying cry to stay engaged, they also convey a substantive claim. In contrast to Michael Walzer's definition of resistance as discrete action, I want to suggest that "sacred" resistance is a stance, a way of being in the world, and an ongoing orientation to the world. As followers of Jesus, sacred resistance is at the heart of our *being*, not just our *doing*.

This does not mean that we go around being "defensive" all the time. It doesn't mean that we will always be angry and argumentative. Rather it means that, as those formed in and by relationship with Christ, our very being is turned toward God and attuned to God's wisdom and way. Therefore, our inward posture centers on

God and resists all that is *not* God, resists all that is counter to the ways of God revealed through Jesus.

Of course, we get turned around and find ourselves upside down all the time. The point is not that we claim to get it right. The point is that, as those who are in Christ, our call is to be deeply, profoundly *with*—with God, with other people, and with all the creatures of the world. As followers of the God whose life is poured out *for* others to bring about wholeness, our call is to find meaning and purpose in doing the same.[3]

This, then, is our way of being in the world: to be with and for God and others and to participate in God's life of love, justice, and mending. In the traditional language, life is found in loving "the Lord your God with all your heart, and with all your soul, and with all your strength, and with all your mind; and your neighbor as your-self" (Luke 10:27). Even our faint and faltering attempts at doing this reveal that, by God's grace, we have already resisted temptations to make our lives small and selfish. We have welcomed the work of Spirit within, work that constantly reforms our hearts and minds, draws us more deeply into God's grace, and nudges us to act. The nature of our *being* necessarily affects and directs the focus of our *doing*.

Our resistance is "sacred" because it is driven not primarily by self-interest or fear or even only a benevolent wish for the good of an oppressed group. It is "sacred" because it is driven by God at work in and through us. It is "sacred" because it is grounded in God's vision of wholeness—a wholeness that embraces difference and delights in the surprises of unlikely friendship, a wholeness that calls us to take up the cross, a wholeness that is worth our suffering and sacrifice. When it is God who inspires our action, sustains our action, and provides the ultimate vision that is the goal of our action we are engaged in "sacred" resistance.

"Sacred" resistance is grounded in the promise that we are not alone in this world or in the ongoing struggle for peace and justice, that the mending of creation is ultimately the work of God, and that we are simply doing our part in the unfolding vision of God's Kindom. Calling on the presence and power of God-with-us reminds us not only of our identity and dignity as human beings but also of the identity and dignity of all people. It is both humbling and empowering.

And it is the primary way to keep from losing heart when faced with the inevitable obstacles, disappointments, and tragedies that occur in the long journey toward reconciliation and justice. When we place our hope and trust in God-with-us, we can, as the spiritual says, "keep on a-walkin', keep on a-talkin', marchin' up to freedom land," for we'll know that, just like Moses, we may not enter the promised land, but it stretches out ahead of us just the same because God is able.

Our resistance is "sacred" because it is deeply rooted in the prophetic traditions of the Bible that find their fulfillment in Jesus of Nazareth. Biblical prophecy provides a framework for both discernment and practice of how to live in community with faithfulness and justice. The prophets teach us that to resist one thing is to stand for another. If, as the United Methodist Baptismal Covenant puts it, we are to "resist evil, injustice, and oppression in whatever forms they present themselves," that means, positively, we are to seek good, justice, and liberation.

Lots of folks think of "resistance" as defensive or reactionary. However, "sacred" resistance as I conceive of it is not merely defensive but is ultimately creative. For example, to resist hatred and violence is to make a positive, creative choice for the sake of love and tenderness. Where hatred and violence are consumptive, love and tenderness are generative qualities. In choosing to risk comfort, status, or safety to be in solidarity with another, you participate in God's way, guided by God's wisdom, empowered by God's grace. If you are participating in God's way, you have a share in the creative work because God is always at work creating and re-creating, mending and making new (cf. Isa 43:19; Rom 6:4; 2 Cor 5:17)!

This way of thinking about sacred resistance is far from negative or simply reactive. It is a way of being, grounded in the grace of God, that attunes our hearts and minds to both the beauty of the world and its brokenness. Sacred resistance is a way of dwelling in God that provides both a vision to work toward and the traveling mercies to get there. Sacred resistance moves us to action and holds us in the promise of God's steadfast presence and love as we take risks in solidarity with others.

It is possible that I am simply playing at semantics, trying to dress up a way of life in words that don't fit or that are inappropriate for the occasion. But in the most difficult moments of struggle in this season of American history, *sacred resistance* has been the phrase that—for me at least—captures the heart and wholeness of my faith and gives me both a strong place to stand and the energy to risk stepping out. Those two words hold the scrappy strength and resolute "line in the sand" and "we can do it!" energy of resistance together with the larger vision of God's loving presence and dream for the world. As is often the case, the words of a poet capture the heart of my ponderings:

Each new hour holds new chances
For a new beginning.[4]

What Do We DO?

For those who love God and love others, for those who are angry and fearful, for those who are vulnerable or seeking to wake up to their own privilege, for those whose hearts are broken, and for the overwhelmed and weary, the question is before us every day: what can we *do*? This book is offered as a resource as we seek faithful responses to the complex and bruising realities of this beautiful, broken world.

It is written primarily for church leaders, both clergy and lay, who are trying to discern how to speak, when to act, and what to risk for the sake of God's way of love and justice. It may be that other people of conscience and good will might find encouragement in these pages as well, and, if that is the case, I would be most delighted.

I hope you won't be surprised to learn that there are not "Seven Steps to Sacred Resistance That Automatically Usher in God's Reign." However, I will endeavor to provide both a broad vision and concrete ways to engage in the work of sacred resistance. First I flesh out a vision for sacred resistance, identify resources in the scriptures and theological tradition that provide guidance and rationale for this stance, and reflect on the dynamics and shape of sacred resistance in the life of the church. Then I explore the question of how the church mobilizes as an agent of sacred resistance—both in its *being* and in its *doing*. There will be reflections on discernment, how to choose when to take action, what kind of action to take, and how to guard against falling into the "echo chambers" of our ideological divides. Finally, I will share some thoughts about how to "keep your lamp burning" for the long journey. Your light is needed, after all. It's what you are made for. St. Francis of Assisi once said, "All the darkness in the world can't extinguish the light from a single candle." And that's an encouraging thought.

Chapter 1

SACRED RESISTANCE: CONTOURS AND COMMITMENTS

Sacred resistance is a way of being and acting in the world that is engaged with and for the world God loves.

Sacred resistance is fueled and guided by a loving God who is the source and sustainer of all life, a God who is always working for good in the world, a God who has been revealed as God-with-us, a God who invites us to share the divine life of creative, mending, saving love.

Sacred resistance is anything—any word, deed, or stance—that actively counters the forces of hatred, cruelty, selfishness, greed, dehumanization, desolation, and disintegration in God's beloved world.

Sacred resistance is nonviolent and seeks the common good.

Sacred resistance "reads the signs of the times" through the lens of biblically and relationally grounded faith to discern how to be actively engaged with the world and to be vigilant against whatever threatens the world's life.[1]

Sacred resistance takes shape in personal attitudes and in communal protest, in spiritual practices and in political advocacy, in how we spend our time and for whom we will risk our safety.

1

Sacred resistance will look different in different contexts because its practitioners will engage the specific situation or reality present at any given time.

Sacred resistance is the domain of no one human sect, faction, party, race, class, or even creed but is primarily the domain of a radically free God who calls us to cross boundaries to share and care for life with and for others.

Sacred resistance is what is needed for the living of these days. And "these days" are whatever days we find ourselves living.

Light and Love

"You are the light of the world. A city built on a hill cannot be hid. No one after lighting a lamp puts it under the bushel basket, but on the lampstand, and it gives light to all in the house. In the same way, let your light shine before others, so that they may see your good works and give glory to your [God] in heaven."
(Matt 5:14-16)

We are light in the world, called to be a shining reflection of the God in whose image we are created. In days when violence and injustice threaten to overwhelm, when the onslaught of terror and grief leaves scant room in our newsfeed for anything else, when we are painfully aware of our smallness and how much we don't know, when what we learn reveals seemingly insurmountable challenges stretching out before us, it is easy to feel that our little light makes little difference. We might experience the flame of our faith, hope, and even love grow weak and dim, challenged as it is by so deep a shadow. This is understandable. Negative voices and energies easily hitch a ride on the shadows of grief, rage, injury, vulnerability, and disappointment.

But in the midst of the shadow, the words of Jesus resound all the more: "You are the light of the world!" *Heeding these words of Jesus is an act of sacred resistance.* In so doing, you resist the temptation to give in to cynicism or to self-protective wall-building or to violent retaliation. To claim that you are light in the world is to receive the good news that you are made to shine, that you have a place and a purpose in the world and for the world, and that your light matters. It is an affirmation that you are a beloved part of God's family, enfolded into God's life and activity. Jesus himself is described as the light of the world, his life "the light of all people" (John 1:4). We are recipients of that light. We are made in the image of Christ. We are to be light for others in the way Christ is a light for others.

Now if that all seems a bit too lofty for a life like yours, then your first exercise in sacred resistance is to take Isaiah 43:1-7 into your daily prayer for at least a week (a month would be even better). Hear these words as God's voice speaking *directly to you*. Listen for what God wants to say to you. Then after at least a week with Isaiah, do the same with Matthew 5:14-16. Hear the voice of Christ speaking these words to you. If you are so led, listen to what God wants to say to you in the longer passage contained in Matthew 5:1-16.

Among the personal messages you will receive, this part of the text is clear: you are precious, beloved, formed and made by God for glory. You are created to share in the life and light of Christ!

There will be those who will reject the notion that sacred resistance begins in prayer or in one person's journey to acknowledge and accept the love of God. What do those things have to do with the heart-rending realities of brutality, hatred, and injustice in our communities and world? What possible difference do they make?

I suggest that sacred resistance begins in the heart of God. It is, in fact, God's consistent stance toward the world. Out of an overflowing love desiring to be shared, God creates the world and all that is. Out of love, God seeks relationship with humankind. Out of love,

God provides everything we need to live in peace, joy, and whole-ness. And when we, God's children, turn away and our love fails, God's love remains steadfast. *God resists abandoning us!*

God could have chosen to let us go. Across the ages, God's prophets are rejected, ignored, or killed. God's people make promise after promise, only to get distracted and wander off into the empti-ness of self-made idols and the conflict inevitably resulting as the fruit of injustice. God loves us and wants to be close to us. We pay lip service to God and want to be close to our stuff. It's an old story that gets repeated through the ages. But the twist in the tale every time? God consistently resists leaving us alone! God chooses to stay with us, to never give up on us, to keep calling us to live into the im-age that is our birthright. God loves us with an everlasting, stubborn love. That love is the model and the fuel for sacred resistance.

It is one thing to believe that God loves the world. It is quite another to allow God's love to penetrate our own heart and life such that it grounds our thoughts, perceptions, and actions.

When you are able to stay connected to the love of God who holds you, calls you by name, forgives you, and empowers you to shine, you will be better equipped to act in the world with sacred resistance. Because you will know firsthand what sacred resistance is really about: it's about love, love that looks upon each person with a desire for their well-being, love that looks upon human commu-nity with a desire for healing and peace with justice, love that looks into all creation with a desire for mending and reverence, love that is compassionate and merciful, love that is stubborn and sacrificial. This is how God loves the world. This is how God loves you. This is how God created you to love.

"You are the light of the world," Jesus says. As long as you take those words seriously, even when you feel dimmed by weariness and worn down with grief, God's love will continue to shine, lighting the way not only for you to keep going but also for others to see you and to follow.

With Others

Twitter is a fascinating phenomenon on the social media landscape. It's amazing how much can be communicated in such a limited number of characters. Perhaps it is the terse nature of the medium that creates opportunity for the pointed and piercing attacks between people that so often appear on my Twitter feed. My strategy has been to pick up news and follow the general trend of social energy on that platform but to avoid getting into "conversations" on Twitter. The few times I broke that rule, it didn't end well. However, one exchange was interesting. This is how it went:

Me: Jesus didn't come 2 disturb the peace of a peaceful world. He came 2 disturb the injustice of an unjust world. #Sanctuary #BlackLivesMatter

Unknown Tweeter: Jesus should really stop the violence.

Me: That's our part of the deal. As Teresa of Avila says: Christ has no body now but yours...

Unknown Tweeter: Can one man tackle the problems of this cruel and evil world?

Me: No. It's the work of the whole body—every member of the human family. Not all accept that work. But we who long 4 love & justice do our part.

Unknown Tweeter: Touché

You are the light of the world. I am the light of the world. All are created to be light, to embody love in action. As the brief Twitter exchange above reveals, there is a strong tendency these days to perceive everything through the lens of the individual (can *one person* tackle all the problems?). But our faith is clear: we do not shine alone.

Sacred resistance is about relationship from start to finish. It begins in relationship with God and is given shape through God's love for each one of us. It is lived out most fully in relationship with and for others. Jesus has no body on earth but the body of people who seek to live according to God's wisdom and way, who seek to make God's love incarnate. The sixteenth-century nun and mystic Teresa of Avila, wrote:

> Christ has no body but yours,
> No hands, no feet on earth but yours,
> Yours are the eyes with which he looks
> Compassion on this world,
> Yours are the feet with which he walks to do good,
> Yours are the hands, with which he blesses all the world.
> Yours are the hands, yours are the feet,
> Yours are the eyes, you are his body.

This doesn't mean that each of us is to do all the work of Christ on our own. The "yours" of which Teresa speaks is a collective. The body of Christ is not one person but is, rather, the whole people of God. When each one of us does our part, shining our light as God has guided us to do, we participate in the ongoing work of Christ in the world. We undertake the work of sacred resistance *with God and with other people.*

This is profoundly good news as we look and see the depth and breadth of suffering and injustice in this beautiful, broken world. It is not up to us to save the world! Salvation is God's work, and we participate with many others to share the divine work of mending.

In our society, folks struggle to get by—to find sufficient economic, physical, and emotional resources to care for themselves and their families. Sacred resistance is not something "piled on" to an already overburdened life but instead an invitation to participate with others in both giving and receiving support and encouragement. As theologian Douglas John Hall writes: "The importance of the corporate nature of the Christian life—the 'body'—lies not only in its meaning for the individuals who are part of it, but in the promise that it provides for their shared work of world-mending."[2]

Thanks to the window of Facebook, I have a view of friends who are not connected to a faith community. Many long for connection to others with whom to process what is happening in society or in their lives. Recently, one of those friends put out a call for people who meet together and discuss "what is going on and what we can do." I thought to myself, "That already exists in churches and synagogues all over the city!" I invited my friend to check out what was happening at the church I serve. One of the great gifts of our faith is that we are blessed with the gift of community, a community that can not only share the work but also expand our perspective through real, honest relationships—and all undergirded by the love and grace of God.

What Others Are We With?

As members of the body of Christ, we are given eyes to see that there really is no "us and them." There is only "we." Jesus came to save not one part of the world but the whole world. The life together into which Christ calls us is not a vision of an exclusive, separatist club. Rather, the church is a living example and practice ground for how radically diverse humans can journey together in mutual care and friendship as we share God's life of creative, mending, saving love.

The church is *with* its members and with those all around them in their local community and world. Those who seek to follow Jesus and those of other creeds and cultures are "in this thing together." And if the church is truly trying to follow Jesus, we/it will understand that God's creative, mending, saving love is extended to the whole world. In this context, it makes sense that those in the human family who are struggling or experiencing pain or injustice will receive particular attention and care. Even a cursory review of the gospel accounts of Jesus's life reveals that he spent most of his energy in the margins, healing the sick, feeding the hungry, confronting injustice, restoring life and dignity to those for whom these gifts had been denied.

Even so, I have had conversations with church folk who are uncomfortable with the idea that God has a "preferential option for the poor." They feel such a statement is exclusive and limits God's care. I've heard things like, "Don't the rich need God's love and grace, too?" This reaction is akin to the "all lives matter" response to the Black Lives Matter movement. The common factor here is the notion that a focused commitment to one group will diminish the dignity, worth, or care assigned to those outside that group. Such a perspective betrays the belief that there is a limited supply of dignity, worth, or care available. This is not true. God's love and grace are eternal and unlimited. There is more than enough to go around. There is not a limited supply of human dignity or freedom. But the truth is that some people and groups have been denied what is abundantly available out of greed, fear, control, hatred, ignorance, complacency, selfishness, rationalization, and all other manner of human sin.

A perspective that rejects the practice of an intentional and focused solidarity with the poor and oppressed can only thrive in a radically dis-integrated context—that is, a context in which our fundamental interdependence is ignored or denied. Such a perspective is maintained at our peril. As the Rev. Dr. Martin Luther King Jr. reminded us again and again, we are part of one family, intricately connected and ultimately responsible for what happens to one another. God made the world this way, made *us* this way, so that until you are whole, I cannot be whole, and vice versa.

This biblically grounded perspective (e.g., 1 Cor 12) is critically important for the work of sacred resistance. At one and the same time, it affirms the wholeness of the human family and acknowledges that the experience of one affects the lives of all. In his first letter to the Corinthian churches, Paul described life together saying, "Just as the body is one and has many members...so it is with Christ....If one member suffers, all suffer together with it" (1 Cor 12:12, 26b). I'll never forget the moment many years ago when the deep truth of these words pierced my heart. The preacher said simply, "The body of Christ has AIDS." It struck me as never before: *my body* has AIDS because the bodies of others suffer from this disease. What affects one, affects all. This brings another layer of meaning to that central law to "love your neighbor as yourself."

As followers of Jesus, we turn toward the places of pain and suffering because that is what Jesus did and because it is the way of lovingly mending the broken creation of which we are a part. It is the truly human thing to do. Even as we focus our attention on the causes of pain and injustice, take responsibility for our own part in those causes, and seek to care for and be in solidarity with those who suffer, our faith always reminds us that God's saving love is for the whole world. Our repentance in word and deed and our solidarity with the poor and oppressed not only serve to alleviate the suffering of our siblings but also serve the good of all. Our call is to work for the *common* good.

Keeping the Good "Common"

At the most basic level, any impulse or decision to focus on the needs or suffering of others is a form of sacred resistance. Our culture, on the one hand, wants us to believe the universe revolves around our own feelings, needs, or comfort. God, on the other hand, creates and calls us to live with and for *others*, to love our neighbors as ourselves. My guess is that most readers of this book are already committed to the work of solidarity and service. Therefore, the task then becomes trying to engage that work faithfully.

One challenge in our current climate is that with so many groups crying out for long-denied justice, it becomes difficult to keep "the common good" in view. A focus on the common good is not a ploy to deny or minimize the specific, urgent human crises that call for attention. It is, rather, to hold those crises in proper perspective. There seems to be a burgeoning emphasis on discrete "social issues" or specific human "rights" instead of consistent emphasis on a more holistic vision of a *common* good. Add to that the nature of our sound-bite culture with its tendency to boil things down to their lowest common denominator, and the stage is well set for polarized "for" or "against" ways of thinking even among those seeking to forward the cause of justice.

The primary struggle is not between one group or another, but it is a struggle to achieve what is good for *all*, namely, the Judeo-Christian prophetic vision of a world committed to peace with justice and guided by love of God and love of neighbor.

Such a holistic vision is critically important in order to keep from falling into the same "us versus them" dynamics we ostensibly want to break down through acts of sacred resistance. When the perception is that one group's need for justice is more important than another group's need for justice, we've begun to tear rather than mend. When distinct advocacy groups fighting for support and resources begin to lose sight of the larger vision of a truly *common* good, the cause of justice is undermined. When the "enemy" becomes a stereotype, a faceless "other" upon whom it is easy to apply labels like *monster* or *satan*, it is time to pause and recalibrate. What affects one, affects all. The common good can get lost in the struggle between competing needs, competing goods, competing sufferings. The common good can also get trampled as we charge ahead seeking to do what is right.

Sometimes, there are events in our nation or world that rightly draw attention to one place or issue. In those moments, people of faith and conscience will do all they can to respond. But most days, in a land as large and diverse as the United States, there are multiple needs for healing and justice all equally urgent and all occurring at the same time. A later chapter will take up the issue of how to discern where to put our energy when there are so many places and people calling for response. The point I want to make here, however, is simply this: there is no part of the creation that God values above another. God loves the whole world and is always working to bring healing and wholeness into lives, communities, and creation. For followers of Jesus, that is the larger vision that holds and guides our work of a truly "sacred" resistance.

If this point seems obvious within a Christian context, it is likely not obvious as a Christian value to those outside the church. What is most obvious in the public square is that Christian leaders focus on specific issues and particular groups of people with judgment, ignore other issues and groups that merit attention and care, and attack one another within the confines of denominational and ecumenical bounds. The work of sacred resistance will seek both to acknowledge this tendency and to be part of its remedy.

CARING FOR THE GOOD OF ALL

God's Good Will for All

Working for the common good (the good God wills for all creation) involves a commitment to the following practices:

Listening and Humility

You must understand this, my beloved: let everyone be quick to listen, slow to speak, slow to anger; for your anger does not produce God's righteousness. (Jas 1:19-20)

There is nothing quite like the experience of truly being heard. To be heard is to be seen, to be taken seriously, to be recognized as a person of dignity and worth who has a voice and a unique experience of life. Listening to another person is a profound act of care and respect. To listen deeply requires practice and often patience. It is something that is increasingly difficult to do in our culture of noise, distraction, overwork, and overstimulation. Listening takes time and attention. It requires that we focus on someone other than ourselves.

A common practice in group conversations is to go around the circle to share information about ourselves or responses to an idea. Listening is often hampered through this process since folks tend to focus on their own thoughts and therefore miss what others share. Learned cultural dynamics related to social, leadership, and gender roles also complicate the process.[1] Add to these human dynamics the realities of privilege and prejudice, and listening becomes even more difficult. Even when we're trying to create spaces to listen to others, it is a challenge to listen deeply and well.

If we are committed to working for the common good, the first order of business is to listen to the real voices of others. To do this well, here are some things to guard against:

- thinking you can correct another person's experience,

- assuming you already know what another is thinking,

- and imagining you have the answer to the "problem" when it is likely the problem isn't even what you imagine!

Whatever privilege you have—whether that is the privilege afforded by race, education, wealth, title, or role—be mindful of it as you listen to the voices of others. Speak less. Listen more. Listen first. Speak to ask questions that help you listen more fully. Be willing to hear things that make you uncomfortable, sad, or angry. Manage your own emotional response. When it is your turn to speak, do so with humility born of love and self-awareness.

One common pitfall is to approach the work of solidarity and service from a place of unchecked privilege. This affects our ability to listen in the ways I've just described. Vigilant awareness of our own blinders—and that we don't even know what we don't know!—is part of the work of humility and listening. It has been made clear to me over the past several years that folks like me—white, "liberal," educated, well-intentioned folks—can often be the worst perpetrators of paternalism and microaggressions.[2] We think we understand things, that we've done all our work, that reading some books, watching movies, or working in a religious or social justice field releases us from our need for thoughtful vigilance around the dynamics of power and privilege. That simply allows old patronizing patterns to take over. We don't mean to do this, of course. But good intentions don't matter if the outcome is the silenced voices of those who know best what needs to be spoken.

In the current climate, one of the disciplines of listening (in contexts in which mutual conversation is possible, not when a person or group is yelling derogatory or demeaning words at you or at others or threatening physical harm) is to bear with "trigger" words and to seek to hear the fullness of what the other is saying. In interpersonal settings or in places where people are trying to share something of their experience or perspective, it is very easy to simply "tune out" as soon as you hear a certain name, phrase, or word. The hard work is to offer the other the gift of truly listening and to seek understanding even if you end up completely disagreeing with their point of view. The goal is to understand at least something of why they hold that point of view and to maintain a sense of human connection in the midst of disagreement.

We can know these things in our head, but doing them—and consistently—takes practice. As with development of any skill, the practice rounds will include failure. Nobody enjoys failure. However, the most mature, accomplished, inspiring folks I know agree that messing up is part of the journey and that big doses of grace are required along the way. When you slide into assumptions, dominate a conversation, label another person with a generalized stereotype, or engage in other behaviors that undermine your goal of deeply listening, humbly sharing, and staying connected as one human being with another, remember to be gracious with yourself. God is gracious with you and will continue to help you. Keep trying.

Looking for the Human Face in Every "Issue"

"You hypocrites! Does not each of you on the sabbath untie his ox or his donkey from the manger, and lead it away to give it water? And ought not this woman, a daughter of Abraham whom Satan bound for eighteen long years, be set free from this bondage on the sabbath day?" (Luke 13:15-16)

A wise mentor recently reminded me that as soon as a stereotype gets activated, there *is* no more "personal" connection. The person or group loses any sense of personhood and becomes like an object, a faceless thing without history, dignity, or heart. In our focus on "issues" people often get "lumped into" a stereotyped identity or perspective. People become faceless blobs in an amorphous, ideological "issue." I can't count the number of times a lesbian or gay friend has said, "I am not an 'issue'!" While sacred resistance will certainly be involved in issue-related advocacy, it is driven by love and relationship.

No human being is an "issue" but rather a complex and unique person and a beloved child of God. There are some experiences related to human needs and desires that all (or certainly most) share—things like adequate nourishment, physical and emotional safety, friendship, and the like. But each person is also deeply original, with all sorts of particularities. Some of those particularities have to do with personality, and others are the result of culture, race, family makeup, sexual orientation, gender identity, and more.

Even when we know that intellectually, it is often surprising when stereotypes get obliterated in our presence. I remember the time when a parishioner's testimony in worship did just that. This young man (I'll call him Adrian) stood up and began, "I am from Texas. I am a Marine. I am a Republican who ran for public office in Texas. I am gay. I am a follower of Jesus Christ." For some, there may seem to be little surprise or shock in Adrian's witness. For others—both at the time and even now—some aspects of his identity feel incongruous. Regardless, the "categories" Adrian named only scratch the surface of who he fully is. If we were to assume what he thinks or how he feels about any of the number of issues that immediately spring to mind, we would likely find ourselves surprised.

Why do we struggle to remember that human beings are complicated and should be addressed as such? Why do we forget that human societies are made up of beautifully complicated human beings and are, therefore, also complicated? It is easier for those with nothing to lose in a conversation to focus on a philosophical or theological "issue" rather than grapple with the human faces and voices of those whose experiences throw our tidy ideological systems into disarray. Our laziness and forgetfulness in this regard weakens any attempt at working for the common good. It allows not only for paternalistic assumptions to run rampant but also for the experiences of whole groups to be functionally erased.

In 1989, law professor and civil rights advocate Kimberlé Williams Crenshaw introduced the concept of "intersectionality"[3] as a way to name and begin to address the ways that people—black women in particular—become invisible. For example, when talking about racism, black men are often the subjects; when speaking about feminism, white women claim the focus. Black women experience both racism and sexism but are often the invisible, silent partners in the struggle. Using the language of intersectionality, Crenshaw sought to provide a framework within which the experience of overlapping racial and gender oppression could be more easily identified and discussed. The term, now part of the social justice and advocacy lexicon, has been expanded in ways that allow it to highlight a variety of "intersectional erasures." Crenshaw writes:

Intersectionality is an analytic sensibility, a way of thinking about identity and its relationship to power. Originally articulated on behalf of black women, the term brought to light the invisibility of many constituents within groups that claim them as members, but often fail to represent them. . . . People of color within LGBTQ movements; girls of color in the fight against the school-to-prison pipeline; women within immigration movements; trans women within feminist movements; and people with disabilities fighting police abuse—all face vulnerabilities that reflect the intersections of racism, sexism, class oppression, transphobia, able-ism and more.[4]

This "analytic sensibility" is a tool that can help us remember the complexities of human beings and societies. But as with any tool, it can be used well or poorly. The goal is to highlight a more realistic picture of reality, complete with the incarnate experiences of all those involved—so that the work of justice can be done. It is only with the *common good* firmly in view, however, that we can capitalize on the full power of Crenshaw's insight. "Privilege checking" within advocacy communities might be a helpful practice if done in love and with grace, but often it can become its own form of stereotyping and bullying. Having said that, it is absolutely critical for those with any privilege to do our own "checking"! Crenshaw names it beautifully, "While white women and men of color also experience discrimination, all too often their experiences are taken as the only point of departure for all conversations about discrimination. Being front and center in conversations about racism or sexism is a complicated privilege that is often hard to see."[5]

In a world that is already so complicated and overwhelming, it is much easier to assign people to a clearly marked "box" and to focus not on real human lives but on disembodied "issues." But intersectional analysis helps open our eyes to see the human faces of *all* those involved in any "issue." It is meant to complicate our perspective.

Therefore, such analysis is a gift to the work of sacred resistance with its commitment to a truly common good.

Keeping Crisis in Perspective

> *God is our refuge and strength, a very present help in trouble.*
> *Therefore we will not fear, though the earth should change, though*
> *the mountains shake in the heart of the sea; "Be still, and know*
> *that I am God!" (Ps 46:1-2, 10a)*

This practice of keeping crisis in perspective can only be achieved in the context of a holistic vision that is truly committed to the common good. Without such a vision, every eruption of new violence or injustice can feel like the end of days. Unmoored from history or context, senseless, banal acts of evil and destruction will tempt us to reactivity—fight or flight—instead of to reasoned, thoughtful, faithful response.

Perspective is how we "hold" reality, how we frame it and understand it. If our framework is God's saving love always at work for the healing and wholeness of the world, we hold moments of crisis differently than we might within another frame. We are reminded that whatever is happening is not "all about me" but is rather part of a much larger experience. We are given the gift of knowing that we are not alone, that God is with us and that there are other people with whom to share the struggle and the work of mending. We will have the benefit of memory—the awareness that the work of cultivating God's Kin-dom on earth as it is in heaven has been ongoing from the very beginning. We will have at least a vague sense of where our energies should be directed (those most adversely affected by the current devastation). These are only some of the benefits of the spiritual practice of keeping perspective. This practice is only possible insofar as we stay connected to a larger, holistic vision. Staying connected requires the help of others who share the vision (community!), regular engagement with the rituals and narratives of our faith (worship and study!), and close contact with the God whose grace beckons us toward the vision in the first place (prayer!).

Another aspect of keeping perspective is the whole issue of "the forest and the trees." Where do you focus attention? Do you tend to the diseased tree in front of you, or do you direct your energies toward finding the root cause of the disease? I think of this as the "levels" of sacred resistance. In every moment of social crisis, there will be a need for immediate care for those directly affected *and* a need for ongoing discernment and dismantling of the deeper issue that is the source of dis-ease.

Years ago, I remember reading about folks who criticized Saint Teresa of Kolkata for her focus on those who were dying in the streets. The critique was that time and resources would be better spent working to dismantle the economic, religious, political, and social systems that left so many in that desperate situation. When faced with this argument, she would often tell of a man who'd suggested she could do more for the world by teaching people how to fish rather than by giving them fish. "The people I serve are helpless," she told him. "They cannot stand. They cannot hold the rod. I will give them the food and then send them to you so you can teach them how to fish."[6] Mother Teresa was clear about her calling to direct service with those in abject suffering. She was also clear that there was a need both for the direct care offered through her work and for those who were called to address the source of the crisis through advocacy, policy, and other systemic change.

In the context of sacred resistance, part of keeping perspective is to be clear about what role God is calling you to play. Nobody can attend to all the needs all the time. In the congregation I serve, there are ministries that provide direct care and service—food, clothing, assistance obtaining identification documents, and so on. There are also ministries that focus on broad-based organizing and advocacy to effect change at the macro level. Our Sacred Resistance Ministry Team has called for actions that were both direct practices (recycle!) and part of more systemic initiatives (call your senator!). We also have study groups, forums, and Bible studies that provide guidance, challenge, and encouragement for the ongoing work. Different people engage in these different ministries, each person filling the roles required to make them happen. All the ministries are important; all the roles are necessary. Remember that you are part of a community, the body of Christ, and if you discern and do your part, you may inspire others to do the same. Something might really change!

Another piece of keeping crisis in perspective is to guard against what my colleague calls "policy by Twitter." Deacon Ben Roberts, director of social justice ministries at Foundry UMC in Washington, DC, defines "policy by Twitter" as "unsustainable, reactionary, and opportunistic responses to real social challenges that only last for a short period of time and rarely result in a solution to the original problem." In our zeal to want to respond, we can lose perspective and begin to think that a "Tweetstorm" using the hashtag du jour will make a substantive contribution toward alleviating injustice or creating positive change. There are a handful of public figures for whom that strategy might work. But for the rest of us, such a tactic may lead to a sense that we have done something meaningful for the common good when all we have done is convince ourselves that we're "woke" as we move on to the next item on our to-do list and wait for the next opportunity to join the social media fray. This is not to suggest that our words and public stance are unimportant, but rather that we need to keep proper perspective about what is happening, what role we are called to play, and if and how our public engagement will effect any positive outcome.

The deadly "Unite the Right" rally organized by white nationalist Richard Spencer[7] in Charlottesville, Virginia, happened during the writing of this manuscript. In its wake, a Facebook post from Chris Newman, a Charlottesville man who describes himself as "your local black farmer," went viral. Newman did not praise those involved in the counterprotests in response to the white nationalists carrying torches. Rather, he called out the pervasive segregation and racial profiling he experiences in the community on a regular basis and the ways these realities affect his business and daily life. Newman didn't mince words when naming the hypocrisy of the city's progressives who assume the race problem has nothing to do with them, but only to do with Confederate flag-wavers. His request was simple: put down the vigil candles and take up the work of dismantling racism in Charlottesville.[8]

Keeping the crisis in perspective as we seek to serve the common good means not only jumping into the flow of a protest march—though that is certainly a valid and powerful act of sacred resistance. It is also recognizing the larger issues at play, the deeper realities that exist, and our own potential culpability in the ongoing systems of injustice to which a march or protest responds. As followers of Jesus, part of proper perspective will always be to search our hearts for the ways that *we* need to *change*. The question is where and how God calls you to respond, change, engage, study, serve, pray, and advocate so that your engagement in the pressing struggles of our day does more than salve personal conscience or nurture an emotionally satisfying moral outrage. The perspective of God's creative, mending, saving love reminds us of our focus and goal. God's saving love is for the world, and you are part of the world.

Love and Nonviolence

> *"You have heard that it was said, 'You shall love your neighbor and hate your enemy.' But I say to you, Love your enemies and pray for those who persecute you." (Matt 5:43-44)*

Sacred resistance does not seek the destruction of perpetrators of harm. Rather, we seek their restoration to the dignity of living in ways befitting of those made in the image of God. This is a powerful and difficult implication of working for a truly *common* good according to the wisdom and way of God revealed in Jesus. Not only are we called to love those who suffer at the hands of oppressors but we are also called to love the oppressors (Matt 5:43-48). It is instructive to remember that love in its most basic Christian form is not a warm feeling toward another (though that is certainly part of many love relationships), but rather it is an active expression of care and reverence for life. We love the oppressor not by liking them personally but by naming their inhuman, unjust actions and attitudes and challenging them to repent—literally to turn around and do what is loving and just.

The debates about whether resistance requires violence are well documented and need not be recounted here. Thoughtful and sophisticated thinkers disagree on this issue, and people of faith must decide where to stand. I am persuaded by those who insist upon nonviolence as the mode by which followers of Jesus resist.

What does Jesus teach us about violence? Jesus's proclamation of the Kin-dom is nonviolent. All his recorded words and especially those in the Sermon on the Mount (cf. Matt 5), his engagement throughout his life with those who would do him harm, and the way he entered into his suffering and death teach and embody nonviolence. Folks may try to challenge this by pointing to a scripture here or there—perhaps a parable that ends with gnashing of teeth or a hyperbolic teaching about bringing a sword. But I can't imagine any scenario in the Gospels in which Jesus did or would advocate doing violence to another person. Can you imagine Jesus carrying a weapon? Can you imagine Jesus beating the body of another person? Can you imagine Jesus calling for an airstrike?

A key scripture is Matthew 5:38-42, a teaching from Jesus's Sermon on the Mount:

> You have heard that it was said, "An eye for an eye and a tooth for a tooth." But I say to you, Do not resist an evildoer. But if anyone strikes you on the right cheek, turn the other also; and if anyone wants to sue you and take your coat, give your cloak as well; and if anyone forces you to go one mile, go also the second mile. Give to everyone who begs from you, and do not refuse anyone who wants to borrow from you.

Here, Jesus references Hebrew scripture, what is known as the *lex talionis*, or the law of retaliation. This was a law designed to regulate justice in ancient Israel (e.g., Deut 19:21). When harm was committed, the Israelite judges were bound to ensure that the penalty was not arbitrary or excessive for the crime (i.e., "eye for an eye"). Jesus mentions the ancient law and then overturns it, saying, "But I say to you, Do not resist an evildoer." The Greek word translated "resist," *antistenai*, is most often used as a military term, a way to describe violent opposition to an aggressor. Walter Wink concludes:

> *Antistenai* means more [here] than simply to "stand against" or "resist." It means to resist violently.... Jesus is not encouraging submission to evil; that would run counter to everything he did and said. He is, rather, warning against responding to evil in kind by letting the oppressor set the terms of our opposition. Perhaps most importantly, he cautions us against being made over into the very evil we oppose by adopting its methods and spirit. He is saying, in effect...do not become the very thing you hate.[9]

The examples Jesus gives in verses 39-42 of giving your coat, of going the second mile, of giving to those who beg are culturally specific illustrations of this core teaching of nonviolent resistance.

Jesus teaches and models courageous, active, nonviolent resistance to evil, injustice, and oppression in any forms they present themselves. We are not to be doormats for abusers or to remain in a life-threatening relationship. We are not to passively stand by in the face of injustice. We are to claim our agency and stand strong in our dignity; we are to tell the truth to those with power and to name the pain that we endure or see. But we are not to respond to hate with hate, to violence with violence. Loving our enemies (Matt 5:44) will take many forms, but you can be sure that torturing, maiming, or killing them is not what Jesus had in mind.[10]

Not only is it clear that Jesus never used violence as a tactic of resistance or rebuke but also the core teachings of Jesus are central to the method of nonviolent resistance brilliantly delineated by the Rev. Dr. Martin Luther King Jr.[11] That method has love at the center, seeks redemption and reconciliation, and targets systemic injustices instead of violently attacking those caught up in their wake. The goal is beloved community, a reality only achieved by love and light, always undermined by hatred and violence.[12]

Some people of faith challenge such a commitment to nonviolence based upon the choice of Dietrich Bonhoeffer to join a conspiracy to assassinate Adolf Hitler. Again, volumes have been written on the life and witness of Bonhoeffer, and there is neither space nor need to fully recount the variety of perspectives here. I will only say that Bonhoeffer clearly didn't make the decision to support violence lightly, and he did so knowing full well that he would have to accept whatever consequences—physical or spiritual—resulted from his choice. As Curtiss Paul DeYoung writes, "If a Christian ever chooses violent resistance, it must be done in the manner that Bonhoeffer made his choice—as an exception to the rule in a case of extreme human rights abuses, after all other methods have been exhausted and much prayer has been offered, and with a full willingness to accept the guilt and consequences."[13]

Later in this book, I will offer some reflections about risk, fear, guilt, and being willing to accept the full range of potential consequences for our actions. As a final word for this chapter, however, I will simply offer encouragement and blessing for the hard and beautiful work of sacred resistance. "Paradox Blessing" is a prayer found in *Celtic Daily Prayer*, one of the prayer books that I use regularly. It is a reminder that blessing can be found in discomfort about easy answers, in anger at injustice, and in tears shed for the hurts of the world. These things can be blessings when they move you to act in more loving, compassionate, and just ways. The blessing ends with a reminder that foolishness is a blessing—the foolishness of thinking you can make a positive difference in the world—because that kind of foolishness can lead you to "do the things which others tell you cannot be done." May all these blessings be yours.[14]

Chapter 3
SACRED RESISTANCE: A WAY OF LIFE FOR THE CHURCH

When I have spoken with folks about sacred resistance over the months of researching and writing this book, many have suggested that the topic—and the stance it seeks to promote—is particularly important at this moment in history. I agree that the times in which we live can be characterized in terms of crisis. Politically, relationally, environmentally, morally, and spiritually, there is deep alienation, disease, and brokenness. However, while this moment may be one in which we realize with searing clarity the need for sacred resistance, I assert that sacred resistance is not simply a reaction to some act, leader, movement, or reality in a discrete moment. It is part of the identity—the very nature—of any community who truly seeks to follow Christ. This doesn't mean that congregations will be marching and protesting every week (although there may be times when that is the most faithful response). It means that congregations will cultivate an inward posture that centers on God and resists all that is not God. It means that Christian communities will understand themselves as participants in God's ongoing creative work of love, compassion, mending, and making new. It means that this cultivation and understanding prepare people and whole faith communities to be ready in moments of crisis to discern where and how God is calling them to respond.

In order to accomplish this, it is critical to do intentional, deep work of spiritual formation, grounded in the resources of our faith. Theologian Douglas John Hall raises a concern, suggesting that there is "a serious lack of informed Christian leadership helping people to locate in the Scriptures and theological traditions of their faith a rationale for the ethic of resistance."[1] He says that while there are many laypersons who want to engage in resistance, "this readiness to resist is seldom sufficiently informed and empowered by Christian reflection."[2] As a result, he says, congregations and individuals are often forced to look outside their faith for inspiration and resources. My own experience leads me to share Dr. Hall's grief and frustration that so many congregations deny or ignore the challenging and powerful resources informing a Christian sacred resistance.

Recently, I served as chaplain of the week at the Chautauqua Institution (July 2017) and preached each day on themes related to sacred resistance. A couple of months later, a woman who had been present that week approached me at a church meeting for conversation. It was encouraging to hear that she found my sermons helpful. But I was particularly struck when she said, "The people I was staying with were interested in what you were preaching, but I had to give them some background about you and your context—because they didn't understand why you were so fired up." My first response was to wonder what people are hearing and engaging in their congregations. How could people wonder why a committed practitioner of the Christian faith is "fired up" in a time when there is so much division, fear, suffering, and injustice in our society?

Throughout my week at Chautauqua, I received similar feedback—from folks who were confused, angry, or caught off guard by what I was raising or who seemed to have been waiting for someone to speak up and make the connections between the Bible and the impulse to push back on words and actions in the public square that are counter to the Kin-dom of God. What all the responses had in common is that they pointed to an absence of this kind of engagement and discourse in the faith communities represented. Of course, there were some exceptions, and I am aware of many faith communities whose sacred resistance is deeply grounded in prayer, Bible study, respectful conversation, sacrament, and other Christian practices. But this recent experience leads me to think the concern Dr. Hall raises is both fair and instructive for anyone who wants to engage in a truly Christian sacred resistance.

Citizens of the Kin-dom of God

One of the confusing and painful realities in our culture at present is that scripture and theology—the very resources that provide guidance for life together—are interpreted and applied in such radically different ways. We tend to think of this in the dualistic framework of "right-left" or "liberal-conservative," a tendency I suggest is not only polarizing but also paralyzing. It is paralyzing because any movement toward the other pole is regarded as suspect at best, an outright betrayal at worst—and no one wants to be labeled as "sleeping with the enemy." As a result, folks get stuck on the far sides of an impassable chasm. This dualistic framework undermines the interwoven realities of creation, human life, and relationship. It isn't conducive to the church's work of mending. It also tends to prop up a paradigm of churches as equivalent to national associations (such as the NRA, NAACP, NAM, etc.) lobbying for policies and practices aligned with—in the church's case—a given theological and interpretive perspective. That is the way many churches currently engage the secular system (if they engage at all), believing this to be the faithful approach as American citizens who happen to be Christian.

But the extraordinary alternative is for Christian communities to claim primary citizenship not in America (or the nation in which they live) but in the Kin-dom of God. This alternative embodies the way of life in God's Kin-dom in such a way that people holding very different political or cultural perspectives are both challenged and fully received. The law of Moses; the teachings of the prophets; the example of the sages; the revelation of God's wisdom and way through Jesus's life, teaching, cross, and resurrection; the story of early Christian community; and the witness of faithful women and men through the ages provide the vision for how to live together. I have witnessed how studying scripture and practicing the ways of Jesus in community allow folks to live, serve, and discern creative solutions together across all the worldly dividing lines. People who would be written off by one another outside the church find, as fellow citizens of the Kin-dom, a sibling whose pain, perspective, and experience can be a source of both frustration and insight.

To intentionally live as citizens of God's Kin-dom is deeply countercultural and an act of sacred resistance in a world that would ask us to worship idols (flag, money, status) and capitulate to the polarized paralysis of "us versus them." When people begin to ground their lives and commitments, not first upon a secular political platform, but upon the wisdom and way of Christ, old polarities begin to break down, and the capacity for participation in mending and making new is at least glimpsed.

I'm not suggesting that we are supposed to sacrifice our deepest values for the sake of "making nice." What is required is not an "I'm OK you're OK" approach, with no critical thinking, debate, or stand taken on anything. This is the preferred mode of many congregations who would rather "keep the peace" and have warm "spiritual" feelings than engage their faith in such a way that its communal implications and responsibilities are acknowledged and owned. That kind of attitude can be held by anyone and *is* held by countless people both within and outside the church. Rather, I am saying that those serious about following Jesus are required to remember that there is an alternative framework within which to understand and live our lives in community with others, even with those members of the human family who challenge us most. In other words, we as Christians are called to the difficult task of showing the world that "us versus them" isn't the only way to live.

The call to claim our primary citizenship in the Kin-dom of God is not to suggest that congregations ignore or withdraw from the pressing matters of the day, but rather that engagement be fueled by the ongoing, deep, difficult, intentional work of seeking to know and love God and know and love others in community. Churches have the resources at hand to engage this work through relationships, study, service, stewardship, and sacrament. The church that trusts God's wisdom and way for its life together and its engagement in the world seeks to be visible as a real alternative. As Stanley Hauerwas and William Willimon write, this church seeks

> a place, clearly visible to the world, in which people are faithful to their promises, love their enemies, tell the truth, honor the poor, suffer for righteousness, and thereby testify to the amazing community-creating power of God.... [This] church can participate in secular movements against war, against hunger, and against other forms of inhumanity, but it sees this as part of its necessary proclamatory action. This church knows that its most credible form of witness (and the most "effective" thing it can do for the world) is the actual creation of a living, breathing, visible community of faith.[3]

Old Testament scholar Walter Brueggemann says something similar as a result of his deep study of the prophetic tradition. He writes:

> Prophetic ministry consists of offering an alternative perception of reality and in letting people see their own history in the light of God's freedom and will for justice. The issues of God's freedom and [God's] will for justice are not always and need not be expressed primarily in the big issues of the day. They can be discerned wherever people try to live together and show concern for their shared future and identity.[4]

The church that seeks to align its identity and practice internally and externally with the ways of God's Kin-dom will not be immune to the challenges that plague human consciousness, relationships, and society. There will continue to be debates, hurt feelings, misunderstandings, injustice, and bad behavior. But a Kin-dom-aligned church will at least know how to identify and respond to those challenges from a biblically rooted, theologically sound, sacramentally fueled, and therefore hopeful and graceful, perspective.

The shape of any given church forms disciples according to that shape. The worship, language, theology, practices, systems for ministry, and stance with and toward others form certain *kinds* of Christians. As a result, if Christian communities understand sacred resistance as integral to the shape of their shared life—even if the phrase *sacred resistance* is never uttered—people will be formed in the ways of the Kin-dom. In days of relative peace, these Christian communities train like athletes in the ways of love, compassion, humility, mercy, and justice. Then, when the hounds of hell do their worst, members of these churches are equipped and trained in God's ways and can discern wisely and act courageously. The bonus is that, even in more mundane moments of challenge—say around the family dinner table, in rush hour traffic, or at the customer service counter—the same gifts of spiritual formation guide and ground our posture and response.

I imagine most churches, if asked, would claim they seek to align their way of life with the ways of God's Kin-dom. And yet so many "church people" are surprised to hear a preacher who is "fired up" that the prophetic, countercultural call of the gospel doesn't seem to take concrete shape in many churches. If churches are seeking to live as citizens of God's Kin-dom, then why are so many Christian people barely distinguishable from anyone else in their values and priorities? I will attempt to address at least some of this in a later chapter, but, for now, it is important to highlight briefly one of the defining features of life in God's Kin-dom.

Cross-Shaped Community

Sacred Resistance begins in the heart of God and is God's consistent stance toward each one of us and toward the world. God resists every opportunity to leave us alone or give up on us. From the very beginning of salvation history, God loves us with an everlasting, stubborn love and is willing to go to extremes to prove it. Paul writes that God's love for us is proven "in that while we still were sinners Christ died for us" (Rom 5:8).

In many churches, the cross is seen as having more to do with "getting into heaven" and "personal salvation" through forgiveness of sins than solidarity with others' suffering or systemic sins or sacred resistance. Therefore, many will hear Romans 5:8 as "Christ died for *me*." It is true, of course, that Christ died for me. I rely on God's life-saving grace and mercy and give thanks for it every day. But Christ also died for you *and for all that is*. The saving work of God is much larger than the sum total of "sin-saved souls." Is God's saving work not also present, for example, in the reconciliation between people or in the healing of bodies and spirits or in making peace with justice? I hasten to add, the work of salvation is also not limited to a social justice agenda—an unfortunate reduction made by many who are either reacting against the prior error or who, for a variety of reasons, wish to ignore or downplay the real and active presence of God.[5] Theologian Letty Russell succinctly provides a more holistic vision, saying, "salvation ... is a word that describes God's mending and reconciling action in our lives and in the whole of creation."[6] The saving work of God is both deeply personal and encompassing of all things.

Jesus the Christ shows us God's salvation; Jesus embodies the saving love, wisdom, and way of God. The world rejected God's way, rejected God's love, and pierced God's heart. We are called to follow the rejected, crucified One. From the beginning this call has been deeply countercultural. As Paul states, "Christ crucified [is] a stumbling block to Jews and foolishness to Gentiles" (1 Cor 1:23). Living as citizens of the Kin-dom means we create a community of the cross. This is one way we embody sacred resistance.

Stanley Hauerwas and William Willimon write:

> The cross is not a sign of the church's quiet, suffering submission to the powers-that-be, but rather the church's revolutionary participation in the victory of Christ over those powers. The cross is not a symbol for general human suffering and oppression. Rather, the cross is a sign of what happens when one takes God's account of reality more seriously than Caesar's. The cross stands as God's (and our) eternal no to the powers of death, as well as God's eternal yes to humanity, *God's remarkable determination not to leave us to our own devices.*[7] [italics added]

The stubborn love of God is powerfully, painfully displayed on the cross. God resists abandoning us even to the point of death. The cross is both nonviolent protest against the death-dealing ways of empire and solidarity with "the crucified people" of every age. The church of Jesus Christ, as a community of the cross, is inherently a community of sacred resistance. We can (and do) ignore, downplay, or misunderstand this core piece of the church's identity and responsibility out of weariness, fear, complacency, or privilege. But it remains the case that following the crucified one connects us not to the powerful but to those who suffer, who "hunger and thirst for righteousness" (Matt 5:6), who are downtrodden and alone. The cross is a constant reminder of and entry point into the deep pain of the world, pain caused in large part by those who abuse their privilege and power.

The cross stands at the center of the church as a constant reminder of God's love and what God has done for us. Because of the cross, we know who God is. We also know who *we are.*

Because of the cross, we know we are those capable of doing great harm and utterly rejecting the truth. Because of the cross, we know we are loved and forgiven; we know we are promised liberation and new life. Because of the cross we know we are part of a whole creation deemed by God to be worthy of such a sacrifice. Because of the cross we know what we're made for and with whom we are called to stand. Because of the cross, we know who we are.

Be Who You Are Called to Be

The cross shows us both the best and the worst we are capable of as human beings.

Jesus shows us our human capacity to love fully, sacrificially, and to stand in solidarity with the poor and those downtrodden by human systems. Jesus shows us our human capacity to do what it takes to live in peace and to embody justice. Jesus shows us our human capacity to forgive. On the cross we see our human capacity, modeled in its fullness by Jesus, to do the hardest thing—not for our own sake, but for the sake of the greater good. This courageous love is the image in which we are created.

But the cross also stands in our midst as a symbol revealing our worst human potential: to lie and deny, to betray another's trust and love, to sacrifice someone else to save our own hide, to remain silent in the face of injustice. The cross shows us our capacity to treat other human beings as objects, stripping them of their dignity and voice. The cross shows us our own potential for cruelty—cruelty of the worst kind—to mock, humiliate, torture, taunt, and kill. This is a betrayal of our true call and is beneath the dignity of creatures made in God's image of love.

It is appropriate for us to feel gratitude and grief for what Jesus has done for us. Jesus has shown that God is with us in our deepest suffering. Jesus has shown us the fullness of God's love "even while we were yet sinners." Jesus has shown us that no sin—even the worst we can do—is beyond redemption, no sin too powerful to be forgiven in God's great love. But if we stop at gratitude and grief for what Jesus has done for us we miss the part where we acknowledge our own responsibility and response. We miss the part where we step more fully into our God-given image and call to resist. We miss the part where we acknowledge who we are created to be, who we are.

Right now, in our nation and in places around the world, the very worst human capacity is on display: cruelty that is not only tolerated but also celebrated, injustice that is not only harbored but also legislated, racism that is not only denied but also defended. Refugees fleeing in terror are turned away by the thousands. Bombings, mass shootings, and domestic abuse are simply part of the daily headlines. We miss the point if we look at the cross and don't see who is hanging there. Jesus isn't alone on the cross. Christ is on the cross with the suicidal youth who thinks that, because he is gay, it is better to die than to live, with LGBTQ people who are scorned and judged and beaten up and killed. Jesus is on the cross with the thousands of unhoused people all over the world. Jesus is on the cross with the mentally ill who have been abandoned to the streets or to prison. Jesus is on the cross with the poor and unemployed. Jesus is on the cross with those enslaved in the sex trade and other forms of human trafficking. Jesus is on the cross with black siblings who—just as he was—are arrested on trumped-up charges, brutally beaten by authorities, humiliated, spat upon, and sentenced to death. Jesus is on the cross with those who are persecuted for righteousness' sake, who put their lives on the line for the sake of others and the cause of right.

It is appropriate to express gratitude and grief for Jesus's death out of love for us. It is appropriate to give thanks for God's saving grace and mercy for "me." But God help us if we stop there. We are called to be and to become more truly human in the image of Christ. And that means we are called to offer our lives for others. We are made—like Christ—for solidarity, love, and justice. Pray that Christ will give you the grace to recognize your complicity with crucifixion, your complicity with putting or keeping people on the cross. Strengthen your resolve to do what it takes to stand in solidarity with crucified people and to tear down crosses and the systems that mass-produce them. Practice deeper listening, humility, and compassion. Pray that the love born in Jesus's flesh might inhabit your own.[8]

It is that love you are made to embody, that is our true capacity and calling. As followers of the crucified one, our call and identity is love, mercy, solidarity, and justice. We can turn away from this call out of fear or selfishness, we can live smaller lives than we're made for, and we can reject the love that forms and fuels a life that is truly human. That is our prerogative.

But thanks be that it's God's prerogative to have mercy on us. Thanks be that in Jesus we meet our God who is radically free and will not be compromised or silenced or co-opted to serve selfish, oppressive, violent human desires. Thanks be that our God hangs in there with us even when we want to trade God in for another model. Thanks be that our God is love and compassion. Thanks be that, even with so much evidence to the contrary, humankind is created in the image of that God. Thanks be that Jesus took the form of a humble, human servant so that we might take the form of a loving, merciful God.

Go Deep

In these pages, I have dipped a toe into the nutrient-rich stream of biblical and theological teaching about the identity and call of the church and those who call themselves Christian. I have suggested that sacred resistance is not just an activity of the church but is part of the core identity of the church. I've insisted that deep and intentional engagement with the resources of Christian tradition—such as Bible study, spiritual practices, service, and sacrament—will both ground and guide the work of sacred resistance. And I've offered a primary framework of citizenship in the Kin-dom of God with the cross at the center as a clarifying vision and clarion call for the churches. There is much more than can be said about all these things; hundreds of books are written on these subjects. The waters of the stream run deep. Part of my hope is that, if you feel called to sacred resistance, you will make a commitment to deep study and engagement in Kin-dom-shaped, cross-informed relationship and community as part of that call. For I fear that, without such a commitment, resistance becomes susceptible to reactivity, judgmentalism, violence, and atrophy. In a world parched for hope, justice, and love, Jesus offers us an alternative when he says, "those who drink of the water that I will give them will never be thirsty. The water that I will give will become in them a spring of water gushing up to eternal life" (John 4:14). Drink deeply.

Chapter 4

PROPHETIC GUIDANCE FOR THE LIVING OF THESE DAYS[1]

No matter the century or circumstance, human conflicts and struggles grow from the same roots. Christian tradition names these roots the seven deadly sins: pride, greed, lust, wrath, gluttony, envy, and sloth. I don't want or need to outline these destructive aspects of human experience here. Rather, I bring them up to highlight the observation that whether it is Israel in the eighth century BCE or the United States of America in the twenty-first century CE, human sin is human sin; and the temptations we face as people and as communities are strikingly alike. They are, with rare exception, grounded in one of those deadly sins.

The primary way human temptation and sin organizes itself communally is through what some call "empire" and others call "the domination system." Scripture reveals that a primary way God engages this communal or systemic sin is through the work of prophecy. Prophecy is central to the work of sacred resistance, and, as such, it is important to understand what prophecy is and what it means to be prophetic.

In the fantastic 1987 film *The Princess Bride*, self-proclaimed genius Vizzini says for the umpteenth time, "Inconceivable!" and so-bered-up, revenge-seeking swordsman Inigo Montoya replies, "You keep using that word. I do not think it means what you think it means."

The word *prophetic* gets used a lot these days, assigned to all sorts of words and actions. Sometimes I wonder whether that word doesn't mean what we think it means. For example, some will say that pastoral ministry isn't prophetic ministry. Some will think of *prophetic* as something mainly done outside the bounds of traditional churches. Others might think of prophetic action as always being driven by anger and public protest; and still others as something that mostly proclaims future judgment.

In order to offer a biblically grounded framework for the work of prophecy—and one that has stood the test of time—I will draw inspiration from the work of renowned Old Testament scholar Walter Brueggemann in his seminal book *The Prophetic Imagination*.

Brueggemann describes what he calls "tired misconceptions" about prophecy this way:

> The dominant conservative misconception, evident in manifold bumper stickers, is that the prophet is a fortune-teller, a predictor of things to come (mostly ominous), usually with specific reference to Jesus.... While the prophets are in a way future-tellers, they are concerned with the future as it impinges upon the present. Conversely, liberals who abdicated and turned all futuring over to conservatives have settled for a focus on the present. Thus prophecy is alternatively reduced to righteous indignation and, in circles where I move, prophecy is mostly understood as social action.[2]

Brueggemann goes on to say that prophecy is both about pointing to a faithful future and about faithful critique and action in the present. But he says that even holding the conservative and liberal tendencies together doesn't capture the fullness of what biblical prophecy is really about. He writes, "The task of prophetic ministry is to nurture, nourish, and evoke a consciousness and perception alternative to the consciousness and perception of the dominant culture around us."[3] To be a prophetic witness is to concretely live, speak, believe, and choose in ways *counter to the dominant culture.* I hope you will notice the resonance here with the notion that the church is called into the alternative, countercultural community that is citizenship in God's Kin-dom. I also hope you see that this definition of prophecy reveals things like practicing Sabbath, tithing, and humility as prophetic acts right along with acts of social justice and belief in a living, radically free God. Brueggemann insists that the most difficult and crucial thing for the people of God to do is to resist being co-opted by illusions, to resist becoming enthralled with the claims, values, powers, and principalities of the world that cannot keep their promises.

Our culture of consumerism, self-help, virtual reality, and might-makes-right is like a siren call that can lure even the most well-meaning among us into capitulation, numbness, and apathy, as if this is simply the way things are and we can't do anything but go along with it. But if we stay awake to these temptations, resistance becomes possible. How do we stay awake? To do so is "exceedingly difficult" according to Brueggemann because of "the immense technological power of the United States" and "the force of homogeneity," a force that is "partly seductive, partly coercive, partly the irresistible effect of affluence."[4] But even so, alternative communities of resistance are still "a thinkable mode of ministry."[5]

In his preface to the revised edition of *The Prophetic Imagination*, Brueggemann outlines the natural habitat from which prophecy may be generated. Namely, prophecy may emerge in "subcommunities that stand in tension with the dominant community in any political economy."[6] There are four things, according to Brueggemann, that such subcommunities will have in common:

- a long and available memory,

- an expressed sense of pain,

- an active practice of hope,

- and an effective mode of discourse.[7]

These four things will provide the broad outline for the rest of this chapter.

Learn and Live the Story: "A Long and Available Memory"

Active participation in a community that tells "the old, old story" not as nostalgia but as a grounding, energizing shared history is a place to start if we want to stay awake to the need for sacred resistance in a culture that would lure us to capitulate to illusions. Brueggemann suggests that a prophetic community is one in which "a long and available memory...sinks the present generation deep into an identifiable past that is available in song and story."[8] This doesn't mean that prophetic witness is stuck in the past, but rather, it means that our story grounds us in what is real, provides a concrete alternative to the illusions of prevailing culture, and reminds us of what is possible through the steadfast, eternal love of God.

On election day 2016, Foundry offered morning, midday, and evening prayer services. At noon, we sang what is traditionally called the *Gloria Patri*—"Glory be to the Father and to the Son and to the Holy Ghost. As it was in the beginning, is now and ever shall be, world without end. Amen." I sang these words every Sunday growing up. The words and melody are so deeply part of me that—like the Lord's Prayer—it's easy to sing without paying attention. But on that Tuesday, singing the familiar words, I found myself brought to tears. What was going on? Hope had touched my heart and mind. All at once, I became aware that no matter what happened in the

41

election, no matter what happens *ever*, the God who is at the beginning of all things *is* now and ever shall *be*. Awareness of the steadfast, eternal presence of God brought (and brings!) the assurance that no matter what mess we humans make of things, no matter how lost we become, no matter how much damage we do to one another and to the creation, God has been, is, and will be at work to restore, renew, resurrect.

This assurance is not just wishful thinking or simple human optimism. Christian hope in the presence and life-giving power of God is based on a lived history of a flesh-and-blood people. The story we tell—a story of a God who creates all that is by the power of a loving word, who draws close to humankind in loving companionship, who is radically free to act in unexpected ways through and for unlikely people, who is passionate and unyielding in the quest to make us truly human (yet always without sacrificing our burden of free will), whose heart is literally broken by our stubborn, selfish rejection, and who has the power to bring life out of death—this story and this God is real, revealed to us through the scriptures, the prophets, and most fully in Jesus. It is our history. It is our story. We are the people of God, the people of this *particular*, historically engaged God. In the present, we hope for the future because we know what God has done in the past.

This is our "long and available memory...that is available in song and story." The past is present as a living memory and as a living hope. Hope in God's loving presence and life-renewing power allows us to believe that things will not always be the way they are today. And our story affirms that as God's people we have work to do as we lean into an alternative future. Hope in a God revealed as with us and for us empowers us to live now in a way that is in line with the Kin-dom vision that will one day be brought to fulfillment. We are to guard against being lulled to sleep or satiation by the sirens of the age. Alert and awake, we are called to live in the hope and freedom and love of God as revealed by Jesus.

We are God's people, people with a particular history, grounded in a peculiar way of being that, from age to age, runs counter to the prevailing culture. The temptation is to fall asleep, to check out, to give in to the self-serving, self-satisfied, self-defensive, self-made ways of the world. But a prophetic community will not allow that to happen. A community committed to sacred resistance will claim the prophetic work of telling a story of love, mercy, compassion, and new life made possible in and through a God who has proved again and again that the way of abundant life is found not in selfish, defensive control, but rather in self-giving, vulnerable freedom. Our shared, sacred story not only gives us solid ground upon which to stand but also provides a community with whom to walk and work and points us, together, in the direction of God's future. That work isn't done only within the confines of faith community but is the work of our whole lives. Communities of sacred resistance can tell the story of God in such a way that we have at least a chance to stay awake.

Lament: "An Expressed Sense of Pain"

Why do we have to feel pain? Our physical bodies are designed to alert us when there is danger; when we touch something hot, pain causes us to protect ourselves. Ignoring chronic physical pain allows whatever is causing the issue to get worse. Emotional pain is less straightforward perhaps, but wisdom reveals that there are similar dynamics at play. Loneliness, betrayal, fear, disappointment, insecurity, guilt, loss, grief—these things have to be named and addressed or the pain of them will continue unabated. We know that denial or suppression of our emotional pain does not make the source of the pain disappear, but rather it can lead to all sorts of nasty, destructive behaviors. For any healing or freedom to happen, we must allow our-selves to *feel* the pain; we have to acknowledge the pain, be in it, go through it. To do so is unappealing, difficult, and scary. We generally don't want to do it. We try to get out of it in all sorts of ways, such as distractions, addictions, and rationalizations.

There is a sinister way in which this human aversion to pain be-comes systemically magnified in human societies. Walter Bruegge-mann describes this as empire, defined by oppressive "rule by a few, economic exploitation, and religious legitimation."[9] And he says that this reality leads to a "numbed consciousness of denial."[10] Bruegge-mann says, "Imperial economics is designed to keep people satiated so that they do not notice. Its politics is intended to block out the cries of the denied ones. Its religion is to be an opiate so that no one discerns misery alive in the heart of God."[11] In other words, the impe-rial reality distracts, rationalizes, and drugs the populace so that the awareness of suffering and human pain won't get in the way of busi-ness as usual and a healthy bottom line for those in the top 1 percent.

Brueggemann insists that part of what it means to be prophetic is to name the pain, to cry out in grief, to allow the realities of hu-man suffering to disrupt the status quo. He writes, "The replacing of numbness with compassion, that is, the end of cynical indifference and the beginning of noticed pain, signals a social revolution."[12] Just as in our personal lives, the beginning of healing and liberation for our communities is to tell the truth, to name the source of pain, to acknowledge that there is hurt, and to begin to address it with love and compassion.

Several years ago my nephew had a poem he wrote selected as the judges' favorite in Fairfield University's annual "Poetry for Peace" contest. The contest draws submissions from students in kindergarten through eighth grade in Fairfield and Bridgeport, Connecticut, and invites the students to write poetry that captures what peace means to them, gathering the winning entries into a book. You can imagine how sweet some of the entries were. A kindergarten class wrote, "PEACE is when we can work together in our class and in our world...PEACE is when we can listen quietly on the learning rug...PEACE is when we take turns and share without being told to." But just when I started feeling sentimental about how wise children are, I came across seventh-grader Skye Green's poem simply titled "Peace":

> My belly starved
> Unhappy, I eat once
> Muddy streams I drink
> Evil invades my house
> Takes me, my sisters
> They slap my mother beloved
> Sorrow, pain.
> Can't do anything
> Dark weeps,
> Gunshots, crying
> "God, why us?"
> Hard life, pain,
> All over again,
> Father died,
> Killed by evil.
>
> I am a man.
> Where's my childhood?

This is prophetic speech. To be prophetic is to cry out, to name what is real in all its messiness and pain and disappointment and anger and fear. Brueggemann suggests that poetry and lyric and metaphor are the primary language of prophecy. Not that we have to be able to rhyme, write poems, or know meter and music to be prophetic. Rather, the point is that the prose style of the day-to-day can become dry and unable to keep us awake. Skye Green and other prophets through the ages get to the center of things, to the truth of things in words that don't go together in the day-to-day way of writing articles, briefs, reports, and action plans.

Think about the prophets in the Bible. They use metaphor and poetry, visual sign-acts akin to performance art, poignant and sometimes piercing words that have at least the potential to shake us out of our comfortable lull. The most prominent of the Second Testament prophets, John the Baptizer, shows up bathed not only in the waters of the Jordan River but also up to his eyeballs in the flow of prophecy (see Matt 3:1-12). John employs the prophetic poetry of the past to point toward God's future—all the while calling people to change their ways in the *now*. And when the Pharisees and Sadducees appear to make a show of their populism, to show that they are "down with the people," John uses a killer metaphor—brood of vipers—to critique and break through their rationalizations.

John embodies and illustrates "prophetic" witness: grounded in and guided by the sacred story, the prophet publicly speaks up—using language that quickens the heart and cuts to the core of things—to name what is real, to critique what is inhuman and unjust in the world, to notice the pain and to give it voice. Prophetic witness will always cry out in grief over the suffering of innocents, the callous inhumanity of so many in power, the greedy destruction of what is good and true and beautiful. Because a prophet looks upon the world and sees beauty and goodness, love and harmony, sees both what is and what can be.

But a prophet also sees that things are so deeply broken, sees that we all participate through capitulation to the culture, and sees that things *must change*. So a prophet will always name *the pain* of our lives and of our world because that is the beginning of social revolution.

A prophet—and, by God's grace, prophetic communities of sacred resistance—will tell perhaps the hardest truth: there is a limit to what we can do as humans. That calls for humility and surrender. In the face of the worst the world can do and in the presence of death, when human powers fail and human community breaks down, God shows up ready to do something new. The prophetic witness—whether that is your own voice or the collective witness of the church—will always say, "One more powerful is coming," one who will gather up all the broken pieces and make us whole.

Imagine the Unimaginable: "An Active Practice of Hope"

How much of your life do you spend feeling disappointed? If I'm being honest, I will tell you that disappointment has been my close companion over the course of my life. I have such high hopes and expectations for people, events, and myself, and things often don't meet my expectations. Human life is always more and less than we hoped for. It's the "less" that we tend to get stuck in.

John the Baptizer, whom we meet in the wilderness in all his dreadlocked, camel-hair-wearing, locust-eating, charismatic, fire-and-brimstone glory, had high expectations and hopes for the messiah. But there's a point in John's story where, from the despair of a prison cell, he expresses disappointment (see Matt 11:2-11). He dispatches some of his disciples to ask Jesus a rather astonishing question: "Are you the one who was to come or should we expect someone else?" In this question I hear subtext: "Should we expect someone . . . *better?*" Jesus isn't the kind of person or leader that John had envisioned, the kind of messiah who would immediately clean things up, make things better, get rid of all the problem people and the injustice of a world not in our control. At this point in the story, John wonders whether his hopes about Jesus have been misguided. I can relate to John's disappointment. For all the years of praying and working for peace, justice, and greater wholeness in the world, it so often feels like the more things change, the more they stay—dreadfully—the same. Are our hopes misguided?

Walter Brueggemann says that prophets challenge that kind of thinking. He says, "It is the vocation of the prophet to keep alive the ministry of imagination, to keep on conjuring and proposing" *alternative* futures.[13] The ways of empire make us feel stuck. The masters of empire try "to banish all speech but their own"[14] and offer bread and circuses to keep people distracted and sated. As a result, Brueggemann says, "We have neither the wits nor the energy nor the courage to think freely about imagined alternative futures."[15] John pointed to a future messiah; and Jesus affirms John's powerful, countercultural prophetic ministry. But even John couldn't fully wrest himself from the *expected* future to imagine what God was up to. Jesus is not the expected "same old, same old" but rather is God doing a *new* thing, something people couldn't imagine would ever happen.

What Jesus reports to John and to us who overhear the conversation in scripture is that he has come to be with the vulnerable, with those who for centuries have little reason to expect that anyone would go out of their way to care for them; Jesus has come in tenderness and love to those who thought their situation was hopeless. Counter to what John may have wanted, there is no celebrity face-off between Jesus and Herod on cable news; no flashy sign of a big ax whacking away at the root of the tree, chaff getting thrown into unquenchable fire, the known world instantly, miraculously sorted into the good, the bad, and the ugly. Instead, simple and amazing things have happened in people's lives, things that bring surprising, unexpected, unimaginable newness.

I wonder whether John could let go of his disappointment in order to see that. As satisfying as it might be for Jesus to have breathed fire in some awesome Raiders-of-the-Lost-Ark-kind of way, getting rid of the chaff in every life and heart, that's not really his style. And, therefore, we learn that's not really God's style. It seems that God insists on taking a smaller, quieter, simpler, more vulnerable approach to salvation.

Jesus comes to human beings—to us—in our need in order to inaugurate a new life. And, if he's paying attention as he sits in the darkness of a prison cell, John just might have the ears to hear this as good news. At the end of Jesus's response to John's initiating question he says, "Blessed is anyone who takes no offense at me" (Matt 11:6). In other words, Jesus says, in essence, "This is who I am and this is what I do, and this is the nature of God and of God's saving grace. Some will find it unsatisfactory and disappointing. But blessed are those who can hear and see the gift being offered."

To be prophetic is to have the imagination to hear and see God's grace and to imagine a world that seems unimaginable—a world where favor falls even upon the meek, vulnerable, and lowly and where love and compassion prevail. If we can't imagine it, how can we work toward it? Prophetic communities of sacred resistance will name the pain of a suffering world but will not stop there. Communities of sacred resistance will proclaim hope even in the midst of all that is wrong. To be prophetic is to let the world laugh at our hope. It is to persevere in peace. It is to trust that new every morning is God's love for us and that all day long God is working for good in the world. To be prophetic is, as prophet/poet Wendell Berry says, to "be joyful though you have considered all the facts."[16]

Energize the Resistance through Peculiarity: "An Effective Mode of Discourse"

When children are tired or anxious or hungry or sick, they will often "act out." That is, their discomfort or need may lead to temper tantrums, defiance of authority, or fidgety activity. The tendency to act out doesn't go away as we age, though it may take slightly different forms. As we mature, self-awareness allows us to manage these reactions a bit better. But the truth is, a "problem child" (of any age) is usually one who has a valid, verifiable need and who simply yearns to have that need met.

Prophets tend to "act out"—not in a childish way, but in a way that intentionally calls attention to places of pain, hunger, burden, or illness. In this chapter, the guiding question has been, "What does it mean to be 'prophetic'?" Guided by Walter Brueggemann, we have learned how our Judeo-Christian tradition inspires prophets to "act out." Communities of sacred resistance who employ "an effective mode of discourse" that is distinctive and energizing "act out" the call and promise of the gospel. Prophets are deeply grounded in the particular story of a God who is love, a God of mercy, beauty, justice, and peace, a God who has a stubborn tendency to act for the humanizing of the world through people others might ignore—folks like enslaved people (Israel) and unwed mothers (Mary). This sacred story provides a concrete alternative to the illusions, empty promises, and inherent violence of prevailing culture, and it reminds us of what is both desirable and possible through the steadfast, eternal love of God.

With the vision and values of this story as a corrective and a guide, the prophetic witness identifies and critiques the inhumanity and injustice of the current reality. To be prophetic is to tell the truth, to name the pain that empire seeks to silence, to allow the realities of human suffering to disrupt the status quo. It is also to see the beauty and possibility of the world. It is to imagine a world that seems unimaginable—a world where favor falls even upon the meek, vulnerable, and lowly and where love and compassion prevail. To be prophetic is to be *countercultural*, to challenge the ways of empire— that is, to challenge oppressive "rule by a few, economic exploitation, and religious legitimation."[17] Prophets and communities of sacred resistance "act out"—not through a temper tantrum, but through the expression of righteous anger fueled by love and the desire for justice—not through mindless defiance of authority, but through principled standing up to death-dealing powers; not through fidgety activity, but through focused organization and action in response to sneaky, systemic oppression.

Prophetic witness is inherently hopeful, for it shatters the illusion that the way things are now will be forever. Prophets are the voice crying in the wilderness of the dominant consciousness, a consciousness that seeks to steal our power. Brueggemann writes, "The [dominant] consciousness leads people to despair about the power to move toward new life."[18] Throughout the scriptures, we see persons and communities who become caught in the dominant consciousness of the time, who become enthralled with the promise of power, or who become paralyzed by fear of harm or rejection. This is our constant temptation and challenge throughout the ages. But the story that grounds and guides us affirms that God is with us, that God assures us we need not fear, and that the God of Abraham and Sarah, of Mary and Jesus, is more expansive than the God propagated by the dominant consciousness. Throughout the sacred story, God's word empowers people to wake up with greater clarity, wisdom, and courage to stand up to the powers that be, to challenge the status quo, to take risks for the sake of love and in the hope of new life.

"It is the task of prophetic imagination and ministry to bring people to engage the promise of newness that is at work in our history with God."[19] We live in a culture that is so susceptible to fear and that, in these days, is vulnerable to despair and "acting out" in all sorts of destructive ways. The ability to be mindful—that is, quiet enough to listen for God's voice—is challenging in this context. But if we are open to receive the word, we are reminded today that we need not fear, that even in the midst of this moment, new life can and will be born; because our God is with us and ignites our power to move toward something new. Even though we tend to simply try to do the best we can within a system that does harm, God is always initiating a *new thing*. God calls us not to wait for legitimation by the dominant consciousness or current system, but rather—in principled defiance—to imagine a new system and begin living in love, compassion, and peace now.

This doesn't mean that we abandon our country or our church. Rather, as prophet and Benedictine nun Sister Joan Chittister says, the prophetic witness is to remain "inside a sinful system, and love it anyway." She writes,

> It is easy to condemn the country, for instance. It is possible to criticize the church. But it is prophetic to love both church and country enough to want them to be everything they claim to be— just, honest, free, equal—and then to stay with them in their faltering attempts to do so, even if it is you yourself against whom both church and state turn in their attempts to evade the prophetic truth of the time.[20]

Brueggemann suggests that prophets stand within the culture and not only critique the present and imagine a hopeful future but also let those things energize ways of being aligned with the ways of God revealed in the tradition, actions that embody our hope for the future, and actions that remain open to the truth that God can always do something completely new.

The Living of These Days

In moments of crisis, much is made of the urgency of response for people of faith and conscience. I am convinced that sacred resistance is what's needed in such moments. One of the constant refrains fueling my own sacred resistance in the days I find myself living are the words of Harry Emerson Fosdick found in the hymn titled "God of Grace and God of Glory":

> Lo! the hosts of evil round us
> scorn thy Christ, assail his ways!
> Fears and doubts too long have bound us
> free our hearts to work and praise.
> Grant us wisdom, grant us courage,
> for the living of these days,
> for the living of these days.[21]

Fosdick wrote these words in 1930, in very different days from those we are now living, amid wars and rumors of wars, excesses and injustices of various kinds, economic depression, ecological devastation (the Dust Bowl), the rise of Nazism, and the peaceful protests against empire (Gandhi). All of this, while particular to the time, is also not so different from the challenges of our own day. Sacred resistance, fueled by and grounded in the prophetic traditions, is what is needed for the living of these days. And "these days" are whatever days we are living. From age to age, human temptation and brokenness leads down well-worn paths. This sense of being doomed to repeat the past might lead some to despair.

But prophetic communities of sacred resistance do not despair—at least we don't get stuck there. In the present we hope for the future because we know what God has done in the past. In the past, God has consistently energized people to listen, to speak up, to cry out, to tell the truth, to imagine alternatives, to stand up to empire, and to act out for the sake of a more loving, just, and human world. Now is our time. And, thanks be to God, the promise is: God is with us.

Chapter 5

STOP SPEAKING "SMOOTH THINGS"

Years ago, I stumbled upon a passage of scripture in Isaiah that, like a red-hot brand from the fire, seared its mark in my mind and upon my conscience: "They are a rebellious people, faithless children, children who will not hear the instruction of the Lord; who say to the seers, 'Do not see'; and to the prophets, 'Do not prophesy to us what is right; speak to us smooth things, prophesy illusions, leave the way, turn aside from the path, let us hear no more about the Holy One of Israel'" (Isa 30:9-11). These words are among many proofs that the human desire to hear only what we want to hear is not a modern phenomenon. Evidence of "spin," denial, selfish short-sightedness, "fake news"—all of this can be found in scripture—and much of it in the thirtieth chapter of Isaiah.

The following pages contain an extended meditation on and exploration of that chapter, focused on verses 8-18. The passage from Isaiah is brought into conversation with Jesus, particularly around the idea of "disturbing the peace." There is much to ponder as we once again encounter the ways that human temptation and brokenness lead down well-worn paths. Going deeply into scripture and trying to listen is one way to counter age-old temptation to stubbornly reject "the instruction of the LORD" (Isa 30:9).

In ----- We Trust

I was the middle child in my family, and both my younger and older siblings lived with significant hearing loss. In our small hometown, the public school didn't have options for any special assistance for them. So my brother and sister did the best they could and found a way to thrive through a combination of lip reading, hearing aids, and lots of hard work. They also found that humor was good medicine. I remember my sister nonchalantly leaning on her hand as she sat at her desk so as to make her hearing aid whistle. The substitute teacher was the only one in the classroom who didn't know what was happening—to the delight of all the kids in the class! They also joked about how handy it was to have the option of ignoring someone with the ready excuse that they just didn't hear. My siblings talk about wearing their aids as "putting their ears in."

If only we could find a way to "put our ears in" so that we might "hear" what God is saying in these disturbing, difficult days. There may be times we would rather find an excuse and remain hard of hearing. But I must confess that I long for a word from the Lord—even though it might be a hard word to hear.

In scripture, having "ears to hear" means more than having physical hearing but rather connotes the ability and willingness to fully receive the message being shared—that is, not only to understand it but also to *take it in* so that it changes our life. And, down through the ages, that ability and willingness have proven to be spotty at best. What makes it so difficult for God's word to get through?

Isaiah 30 is attributed to the prophet identified as the first Isaiah who began his prophetic ministry in the eighth century BCE in Jerusalem after Assyria conquered the northern kingdom of Israel. The Assyrians have turned their eyes south and are coming for Judah just as they did for Israel. King Hezekiah of Judah has formed a military alliance with the Egyptians to try to defend his kingdom, and Isaiah is having none of it. Isaiah referred to the king's negotiation as making "a covenant of death" (Isa 28:15). The prophet writes:

> Oh, rebellious children, says the LORD,
> who carry out a plan, but not mine;
> who make an alliance, but against my will,
>   adding sin to sin;
> who set out to go down to Egypt
>   without asking for my counsel,
> to take refuge in the protection of Pharaoh,
>   and to seek shelter in the shadow of Egypt;
> Therefore the protection of Pharaoh shall become your shame,
>   and the shelter in the shadow of Egypt your humiliation.
>   (Isa 30:1-3)

Why is Isaiah so upset? After all, Isaiah has seen what happened to Israel; he knows what the Assyrians are capable of; he knows that Judah is vulnerable. And it seems Hezekiah—who by all accounts is the first king in ages who is worth much (2 Kgs 18:3)—is just trying to be a good king and find some help for his people. And that, I imagine Isaiah might say, is the crux of the issue: from whom do you seek help?

The prophet sees that, as a nation, Judah is paying lip service to God (Isa 1:11ff.), but when it comes right down to it, it is not God's but human counsel that guides their steps, not God's but human strength they count on, not God's but human ways they employ in their quest for safety and well-being. They know the instruction of the Lord, the commandments to do justice, have mercy, walk humbly, and live in peace, the commandment to love the Lord with heart, soul, mind, and strength and to love neighbor as self. They know that putting trust in mortals—our own strength or that of others—is just another form of idolatry and will not bring the desired result.

This is the people formed through the liberating activity of God who brought them out of slavery, guided them through wilderness, and provided for their needs. The people have heard this instruction, have been given their very lives and identity through that sacred story but—when the prophet reminds them of these things—they don't want to be bothered with the word of the Lord, but instead they choose illusions. They don't want to see what is happening all around them but prefer to keep their heads in the sand. They don't want to walk in the ways that lead to life but instead make a "covenant of death." They want to "hear no more about the Holy One of Israel" (Isa 30:11).

This is the same old story we've heard before; it's history repeating itself. This is the same choice that is before would-be followers of YHWH from age to age. This is Moses sharing the Law (God's wisdom and way) with the people, setting before them life and death and exhorting them to choose life (Deut 30:15-20). This is Joshua encouraging the people to renew their covenant with God saying, "Now if you are unwilling to serve the LORD, choose this day whom you will serve" (Josh 24:15). This is Jesus in the wilderness tempted by the devil (Matt 4; Mark 1; Luke 4). This is you and me every day of our lives. Choose whom you will serve. Choose whom you will worship. Choose whom you will listen to. Choose whom you will trust.

The choice matters not because of loyalty to some trite religiosity—or to prove allegiance to some perverse religious version of team spirit. The choice matters not because God will punish you if you make the wrong choice—though that is part of the interior logic of first Isaiah and many other ancient prophets before Jesus. The choice matters because what (or whom) we worship, where we put our trust, forms who we are; whom we listen to shapes our perspective, our priorities, and our actions. (That is true for our news outlet as well as for our God.) God knows that the choice of whom we worship, whom we trust, has consequences not only for our own lives but for the lives of those around us. From the time of Moses until our own day, those consequences are life and death.

Isaiah called Judah out for putting their trust in "oppression and deceit." To "trust oppression" is to get your needs or desires met through abuse of privilege, exploitation, bullying, and greed. To "trust deceit" is to believe that promoting the false self, lying, and scheming are the most effective means of relationship. If you put your trust in oppression and deceit, what happens to your heart? Your soul? Your mind and strength? What happens to your relationships? And when leaders—those with power and influence—put their trust in oppression and deceit, what happens to the people? We know the answer. It's an old story we've seen over and again.

In his July 13, 2017, column, journalist Michael Gerson describes the result very well. Trusting oppression and deceit creates "an ethos in which victory matters more than character and real men write their own rules." I would add that it also rallies the worst angels of human nature in order to "win," inciting fear, encouraging violence, promoting ignorance, and reveling in the humiliation and oppression of others. Gerson goes on to make this stunning statement: "A faith that makes losing a sin will make cheating a sacrament."[1] There are consequences for where we put our faith.

Power, winning, wealth, fame—these are the promises of idols. And God has been trying to wake us up forever to the truth that these promises are empty, that they cannot be trusted, that any gains will be short term at best, that the cost will be not less than everything. But our culture is saturated with an idolatrous faith that makes losing a sin, whose values are in direct contradiction to the righteousness and justice of God.

The choice between this faith and the faith many of us profess is perhaps most succinctly captured by an old *Pearls Before Swine* cartoon. In the cartoon, Rat explains that he's trying to come up with a motto to live by. Pig makes some suggestions, the first being, "Love your neighbor as yourself." When Pig asks Rat what he's come up with, Rat's answer is, "Crush the little people." Then in the last frame he says, "I'm trying to be realistic."

In our world—and, it seems, it has been this way forever—being "realistic" leads people to put their trust in whatever they think will get them safety, power, comfort, attention, or wealth. Being "realistic" leads us to believe that violence and exploitation are unavoidable. Being "realistic" leads to making "covenants of death" with nations who will not save us and sealing those covenants with oppression and deceit. "This is the way the game is played," folks will say. And the "little people"—the poor, the children, the marginalized—are always the ones who suffer as a result.

Ten years ago, I read that American children spent more than four hours a day in front of televisions, video games, and computers. When I checked the data more recently, that number had doubled to nine hours a day. Out of concern for the effects of mass media on our children, psychologist and educator Dr. David Walsh wrote a book (nearly twenty-five years ago!) in which he identified six key values that dominate the media.[2] It is hard to argue with his list even after all this time:

1. Happiness is found in having things.

2. Get all you can for yourself.

3. Get it all as quickly as you can.

4. Win at all costs.

5. Violence is entertaining.

6. Always seek pleasure and avoid boredom.

This is what's streaming into not only our children's consciousness but also our own every day. These values are the commandments of current cultural religion. There is daily proof that, as a nation, we do more than pay lip service to these commandments. "In God we trust" may be written on our money, but our money serves other gods. There is growing proof that plenty of people who call themselves Christian worship at these altars. And, while you may not consciously profess the commandments of our current cultural religion, it behooves all of us to consider the ways that we remain deaf to the ways our lives and choices have been co-opted by them, the ways we have surrendered before the dogged persistence and urgency of their claims.

The good news is that our God is just as doggedly persistent, even in the face of centuries of willful rejection. Even amid whatever it is that tempts you to dismiss God's prophetic call, "the LORD waits to be gracious to you [and] will rise up to show mercy to you" (Isa 30:18). God is determined to get through to us. God's love for us is steadfast and stubborn. God knows what will happen to us (as persons, nations, world) if we keep choosing to put our trust in idols. God wants to save us from that devastation. And so, once upon the fullness of time, God got up in our face—with a flesh-and-blood face just like our own—to show us that the most "realistic" and powerful and trustworthy thing in the world is love, the kind of love the apostle Paul describes: patient, kind, not envious, arrogant, boastful, rude, not irritable or resentful, not rejoicing in wrongdoing, but rather in the truth (1 Cor 13). *That* word of love drew near to us in Jesus; and denial, betrayal, back-room deals, secret money transfers, mob mentality, violence, and even death were no match.

God's word of saving love is spoken—eternally spoken. Are your ears in?

60

Hear and See

Early in ministry, I was serving as youth minister and was called upon to preach that Sunday's sermon. Phil, one of my youth, approached me, clearly wanting to see me before worship. I anticipated the affirmation and support I'd receive from this kid who'd been with me on a couple of mission trips and was a regular in youth group. I knew he liked me even though he was careful to be appropriately aloof as befits a sixteen-year-old boy. "You're preaching today!" he said. I beamed. Phil continued with these gushing words: "Make it interesting." Such good counsel we receive from our youth—if we have ears to hear.

To "make it interesting," to invite people to receive God's love and liberating grace, to share the promise of sharing in God's life in a way that is not only acknowledged but also heeded and truly received has always been a challenge. In biblical terms, to "hear" God's word means it is received not just as an intellectual assent or emotional response, but in such a way that what we receive adjusts the core of our being, changes our life from the inside out. I believe it was the late William Sloane Coffin who said that the most difficult journey to make is the journey from the head to the heart. New creation is only possible when that round-trip is completed.

Isaiah of Jerusalem fully received God's message; God's vision took root in his heart. That vision is of human community living together in covenant faithfulness, loving God and neighbor, doing good, seeking justice, rescuing the oppressed, defending the orphan, pleading for the widow, and beating swords into plowshares (e.g., Isa 1:17; 2:4). This is the Isaiah who writes the vision we call "the peaceable kingdom" (Isa 11). This vision of peaceful, loving interdependence guided all he saw and heard and spoke.

And as Isaiah looks at Judah in this moment of crisis, he sees them reject that vision and, instead, turn toward "oppression and deceit," making choices that lead to breakdown of community, increased suffering of the vulnerable, and a capitulation to the presumed necessity of violence.

The prophet reminds them that "in quietness and trust" they will remember who is able to liberate them; in returning to God and resting in God, they will be given wisdom and courage for the present struggle. But they say, "No, thanks. We're good with oppression and deceit."

I think of the poignant words of Jesus hundreds of years later saying, "Jerusalem, Jerusalem, the city that kills the prophets and stones those who are sent to it! How often have I desired to gather your children together as a hen gathers her brood under her wings, and you were not willing!" (Luke 13:34).

Why? Why do we reject the words of God's prophets? Why are we so unwilling or unable to receive the word and change course? So often prophetic vision not only calls people back to the promise of God but also has prescience to see the writing on the wall if things don't change. Isaiah paints a picture of a crashed wall, of a smashed pottery vessel. And yet even the announcement of impending utter destruction doesn't make an impact. In fact, the people tell the prophet to stop telling the truth and to quit speaking of God altogether. One translation of Isaiah 30:10 of our text reads, "Don't talk to us about what's right. Tell us what we want to hear. Let us keep our illusions." And my question is: why? What would your answer be?

I imagine that in our overworked, message-saturated culture potential responses include:

- "I want to keep my illusions because I'm tired!"

- "I'm just trying to get through the day, and the struggles of this day are enough."

- "I don't need anything else to do or learn or anyone else to care for!"

- "I'm on information overload and need a break—especially from bad news!"

- "I want to keep my illusions about my life (or my relationship, community, or culture) because the truth is too painful, the reality is too overwhelming.

Perhaps we grow complacent or want to believe that things aren't so bad and everything will work itself out. But this last perspective is only possible if you live in relative safety and comfort. If you don't feel pain or discomfort there'll be little reason to think anything needs to change and you'll resent anyone who threatens your relative ease. That, as you may know, is called privilege. From that place, we are put out by dire reports and predictions and will work overtime to prove them wrong even in the face of verifiable data! Perhaps we want illusions because what would be required of us if we truly allowed God's vision to take root in our heart is simply too costly.

Prophets tend to communicate inconvenient truths that require real change. That happens on both the small and large scale. A teensy example to make the point: there are things I need to change in my life that, if left uncared for, will certainly have negative consequences (rest, exercise, follow up on health insurance benefits, getting established with a primary care physician, having a difficult conversation, and so on). When my spouse has the audacity to speak up and suggest I do whatever the thing is that I know I need to be doing, I want to kill him (metaphorically)! One factor in this response is exhaustion and frustration; I already know I need to do the thing and haven't been able to make it happen. Other factors are guilt or regret. When we don't want to see our fault or failing or frustration, we may

63

lash out at the ones who remind us of it. The result is that we end up hurting ourselves and "rejecting the prophet," the one who insists we do or receive what would be good for us and for others.

Smart, accomplished people who care can inadvertently miss what God is trying to do or say because we think we understand the situation or issue. Without meaning to, we begin to think we can—or are supposed to—handle things ourselves and need no assistance or further word from God on the subject. The best illustration of this I've ever heard is found in the late Rev. Bruce Larson's book *Believe and Belong.* Larson observes that in the entrance of the RCA building in New York's Rockefeller Center is a gigantic statue of Atlas, a beautifully proportioned man who strains to hold the world upon his shoulders. Here's the most powerfully built man in the world who can barely stand up under this burden. Trying to carry the world on your shoulders like Atlas is one way to live. But just across the street on the other side of Fifth Avenue is Saint Patrick's Cathedral, and behind the high altar is a little shrine of the boy Jesus, perhaps eight or nine years old, and with no effort he is holding the world in one hand. We have a choice. We can try to carry the world on our shoulders—all the injustices, insecurities, hurts, doubts, needs, hardened expectations, confusion, cynicism, fears, and anxieties—thinking we know best; or we can let God help us. I can just hear Atlas saying to God's offer to help: "No thanks. I'm good."

Exhaustion, being overwhelmed, privilege, despair, paralysis and struggle to change, and an overactive sense of our own knowledge and capacity—these and so many other things can keep us from hearing or seeing the word of God's saving love and mercy. But the prophets keep trying to find ways to get through, to make it interesting, to get our attention.

I imagine that most of us have heard God's call to love and serve and give and forgive. We have been given glimpses of God's beautiful vision of a world living gently with the creation and one another.

We *know* this stuff. It's one thing to know these things intellectually or feel them emotionally and another for them to change our life. Where are you on that round-trip journey from the head to the heart?

Stop Speaking Smooth Things

"It's poor religion that can't provide a sufficient curse when needed."[3] Wendell Berry said that.

Another poet and prophet said this: "They are a rebellious people, faithless children, children who will not hear the instruction of the LORD; who say to the seers, 'Do not see'; and to the prophets, 'Do not prophesy to us what is right; speak to us smooth things, prophesy illusions, leave the way, turn aside from the path, let us hear no more about the Holy One of Israel'" (Isa 30:9-11).

Speak to us smooth things. What are the "smooth things" that we want?

- Smooth talk, soothing and affirming, leaving us comfortable and sated in our cozy perspectives and opinions and practices.

- Interpretations and sermons that ignore the inherently political implications of the prophetic tradition, a tradition that finds its fulfillment in Jesus.

- Fake news that props up our biases, that nurtures lazy thinking, and that asks nothing of us.

- Be careful never to make us shift in our seats.

- Feed us words that comport with our theological or political or moral platform.

- Give us language for how we can continue to judge others as sinners, as ignorant, as immoral, while never having to acknowledge our own sin and complicity in the things that do harm.

- Speak to us smooth things; tell us what we want to hear.

But God's prophets will not oblige. Strange and provocative, aggravating and inconvenient, painful and convicting, life-changing and mind-blowing—the words of God's prophets are often pretty rough. And they are the words that we not only need to hear but also need to be willing to speak and to live in this world so weary and wounded and in need of God.

Too often people of faith have been unwilling to admit we even *see* the hard thing, much less to name it in a truthful way or risk anything in response. Specifically calling out those in my vocation, the Rev. Dr. Otis Moss III has said:

> Can preaching recover a blues sensibility and dare speak with authority in the midst of tragedy? America is living stormy Monday, but the pulpit is preaching happy Sunday. The world is experiencing the blues, and pulpiteers are dispensing excessive doses of nonprescribed prosaic sermons with severe ecclesiastical and theological side effects. The church is becoming a place where Christianity is nothing more than capitalism in drag....Why have we emphasized a personal ethic congruent with current structures and not a public theology steeped in struggle and weeping informed by the blues?[4]

Moss's words make me think of another colleague's comment about folks who find their way into our congregations after a life of either no religion or a long lapse from it. My colleague said, "They come just looking for fraud." That is to say, people these days don't expect churches to actually have anything life-giving or honest about them. Folks don't expect churches to tell the truth about white supremacy, about our dependence on the military industrial complex, about the indignity of being unemployed or underemployed, about the AIDS epidemic still wreaking havoc in the poor, black communities in the South, or about climate change, crushing loneliness, the booming sex trade in our country, mental illness, the opioid addiction crisis, and on it goes. People these days expect to find in our congregations little acknowledgment of the struggle and confusion and complexity and pain that marks much of our human experience. At best, perhaps, they expect lip service to God's care and love, to peace with justice, to compassion and reconciliation, to resurrection and hope, even to "social justice"—without any verifiable evidence that the words are backed up with action. Across the years, the most common critique leveled at church people is what? Hypocrisy.

I tend to think some folks use that excuse as a way to keep God at arm's length. But, honestly, I understand why people want an excuse to stay away from faith community. Our track record is dicey. And it's been that way since the beginning. Back in the eighth century BCE God spoke through the prophet Isaiah, calling out the fraud of the people's empty worship and ritual, saying, "I cannot endure solemn assemblies with iniquity.... Even though you make many prayers, I will not listen; your hands are full of blood. Wash yourselves; make yourselves clean; remove the evil of your doings from before my eyes; cease to do evil, learn to do good; seek justice, rescue the oppressed, defend the orphan, plead for the widow" (Isa 1:13-17).

Embedded in this critique is part of the vision that sets hypocrisy in sharp relief: "do good, ... rescue the oppressed, defend the orphan, plead for the widow." Not only do prophets provide a critique of the way things are, but they also do so in light of God's vision for how things *should and can be*. We have been given a vision for how to live together in mutuality, trust, reverence for life, dignity, respect, and love. We have been called to be caretakers of one another and of the creation. The prophetic vision provides guidance for how to walk in God's wisdom and way.

For Christians, Jesus shows us what it looks like when God's wisdom and way is fully enfleshed. It is this beautiful and life-giving vision that is our goal—as people and as the human family. When that vision is trampled, ignored, mocked, and denied, it's time to stop speaking smooth things. When the poor and the immigrant are not cared for, when our siblings of other faiths and of other gender identities and orientations are condemned, when our forests and rivers and vulnerable habitats are destroyed, when the sick are told to make the hard decision to give up their iPhone so that they can pay for healthcare, it's time to stop speaking smooth things. When violence and war are constant and cause no public lament or debate but are simply accepted as the natural course of things, it's time to stop speaking smooth things.

Wendell Berry's poetry regularly takes my breath away; the beauty, the pathos, the truth, and the simplicity of Berry's words are powerful. His words are also prophetic. Berry clearly has no use for "speaking 'smooth things'"! An example:

> The year begins with war.
> Our bombs fall day and night,
> Hour after hour, by death
> Abroad appeasing wrath,
> Folly, and greed at home.....
> This is a nation where
> No lovely thing can last.
> We trample, gouge, and blast;...
> Fine men and women die,
> The fine old houses fall,
> The fine old trees come down:
> Highway and shopping mall
> Still guarantee the right
> And liberty to be

A peaceful murderer,
A murderous worshipper,
A slender glutton, Forgiving
No enemy, forgiven
By none, we live the death
Of liberty, become
What we have feared to be.[5]

That was written in 1991 during the Gulf War. It could have been written at any time, during any administration since. A "sufficient curse" is, perhaps, nothing more than telling the truth, holding up a mirror so that we are forced to look at ourselves. That is what Berry does. That is what Isaiah is doing in the words to Judah. The prophet names what is happening, calls out the oppression and deceit of the culture, identifies the people's rejection of God's vision, and writes it down as a witness forever.

None of this matters if, in response, all we do is feel guilt or allow ourselves to become overwhelmed to the point of paralysis. Prophets call us to respond, to turn and to return to God's wisdom and way. Our faith promises that each of us can do something in service to God's beautiful vision for this world. Our faith also promises that God will give us grace, insight, passion, skill, perseverance, love, compassion, generosity; these and many more graces equip you and me, in all our particularity, to participate in God's work in the world. Perhaps most of us will not find ourselves on a prominent public platform to speak truth to power; but all of us can seek to tell the truth where we live. We can seek to live with integrity, to be willing to at least *try* to see and to hear the complex realities around us, the cries for justice, the needs for healing. We can do our best to do more than pay lip service to the commandments to love God and neighbor. We can work diligently to nurture trust and relationship in our faith communities and at least *try* to offer the world an alternative vision to the prevailing culture of polarization and demonization.

What a gift it would be to that person who risks crossing the church's threshold to find not fraud, but a community being honest about their differences, grappling with the real conflict difference brings, continuing to love each other, and working to "maintain the unity of the Spirit in the bond of peace" (Eph 4:3). What a gift it would be for folks to find faith community naming the pain of suffering, injustice, brokenness, and death and engaging in lament. There is something powerful about having our truth spoken in sacred space. There is something healing about seeing honest lament begin to energize loving engagement.

The world is living stormy Monday and longs for shelter from the storm. Hallmark cards, bunnies and flowers, nice words and sentiments, tiptoeing around the issues, failing to name the pain, never asking the real questions, playing church when the poor and oppressed are dying in the streets isn't going to cut it. Stop speaking smooth things. Truth telling and solidarity and devotion to God's wisdom and way may lead to the cross, but we know the story; and—if we're not hypocrites—we'll have the courage to speak and act with assurance that new life is on the other side.

Disturbing the Peace (aka No More "the Way We've Always Done It")

"Do you think that I have come to bring peace to the earth? No, I tell you, but rather division!" Those are words of Jesus recorded in Luke 12:51 and are part of a longer teaching about the way and the cost of discipleship. Jesus isn't messing around! No "smooth word" here. Jesus is clear that our choices have consequences. In a time when we find ourselves so divided, when violence and exclusion, judgmentalism and rancor are so prevalent in public discourse and interaction, the last thing we want to hear is that Jesus—Jesus of all people—is a proponent of division, using images of fiery destruction to describe his activity ("I came to bring fire to the earth" [Luke 12:49]). Can't we just skip this part?

The only easy way out would be to suggest, as some scholars do, that Jesus didn't say these things. The problem with that approach is words like these from the mouth of Jesus are found in Matthew, Mark, Luke, and even the Gnostic Gospel of Thomas. This leads me to believe that we need to pay attention, to sit with any discomfort, and to listen.

A while back, I read through the entire Gospel of Luke to write reflections for the CEB Women's Bible I edited for Abingdon Press. One of the benefits of reading a Gospel all the way through is that themes and details begin to emerge that are harder to discern when all you get are little chunks here and there. A couple of things that strike me about Luke's version of the story: in the midst of the beautiful birth narratives, Mary sings about radical reversals—"[The Lord] has scattered the proud in the thoughts of their hearts. [God] has brought down the powerful from their thrones, and lifted up the lowly; [God] has filled the hungry with good things, and sent the rich away empty" (Luke 1:51-53). We also hear these words from the prophet Simeon to Mary: "This child is destined for the falling and the rising of many in Israel, and to be a sign that will be opposed so that the inner thoughts of many will be revealed" (Luke 2:34-35). It takes no time at all for Simeon's prophecy of opposition to Jesus to be fulfilled: in chapter 4, Jesus gets run out of his own hometown; and in chapter 5, we start to hear about the religious leaders taking issue with Jesus's teaching and healing activity. By the sixth chapter, they are actively looking for a way to accuse Jesus.

All of this is to say, it should come as no surprise to us to hear Jesus say, "Do you think that I have come to bring peace to the earth? No, I tell you, but rather division!" Division, opposition, conflict.

How do these things fit into a faith that we thought was about love, unity, reconciliation, and peace? Didn't the angels sing about peace when Jesus was born? Don't we call Jesus the Prince of Peace? Have we gotten it wrong?

I don't think we've gotten it wrong about love and peace being at the heart of the good news. But I do think we struggle to acknowledge the potential conflict that following Jesus necessarily entails.

I don't know many people who truly enjoy conflict—though there are a few! Most folks I know do anything they can to avoid it. To be "conflict-averse" is common! Churches are notoriously good at conflict-aversion, taking the path of least resistance, failing to make hard decisions or take risks, for fear of losing people or making folks uncomfortable or angry. We tend to be good at speaking "smooth things." Every church gathering I've ever been in chuckles knowingly at the phrase "the way we've always done it." Disrupting "the way we've always done it" is a surefire way to create division and conflict. So it rarely happens.

In our faith communities and in our personal lives the lengths to which we go to "keep the peace" can be stunning. And it really is understandable because conflict is painful, emotionally and sometimes physically. Some of us have had more than our fair share—and for reasons completely out of our control. Conflict can mean that we lose friends or others who are dear to us. Conflict can bring about changes that disrupt what has been meaningful and life-giving in our lives. Why would we do anything that risks having those effects? And doesn't our faith tradition call us to be peacemakers?

While the Gospel does say that the peacemakers are blessed, it also says (in the very next line), "Blessed are those who are persecuted for righteousness' sake, for theirs is the kingdom of heaven" (Matt 5:10). Here is where we begin to understand what Jesus means when he speaks of bringing division. The truth is that Jesus created conflict and that many people were opposed to him almost from the very beginning. But Jesus didn't create conflict simply for the sake of conflict. He created conflict "for righteousness' sake" and was "persecuted for righteousness' sake." Jesus is the fulfillment of Isaiah's prophecy of a just ruler who "with righteousness... shall judge the poor, and decide with equity for the meek of the earth" (Isa 11:4).

Jesus doesn't come into a world that is peaceful or whole or just. Jesus doesn't come to disturb the peace in a peaceful world; Jesus comes to disturb the injustice of an unjust world. Jesus comes to disturb the things of the world that are not resonant with the Kin-dom of God. That Kin-dom is characterized by mutual love, respect, mercy, compassion, sacrifice for the sake of the other, equality, and so on. God's Kin-dom is characterized by justice—not the eye-for-an-eye, retributive kind of justice that we know and love, but rather the kind of justice that is restorative, that is gracious, that is, frankly, quite challenging for most of us in this time and place. Walter Brueggemann (renowned biblical scholar) says that "justice is to sort out what belongs to whom, and to return it to them."[6] The Kin-dom of God is good news for everyone but especially for those who have had what belongs to them taken away—whether that be their fair and equitable living, their dignity, their freedom, or their safety.

If we choose to follow Jesus, there's a good chance we will find ourselves in trouble. But that trouble is for a purpose, for the sake of sharing justice and every other good gift of the Kin-dom. The point is not that we are supposed to go looking for trouble or that we should "stir the pot" for no good reason. Jesus comes to change what is wrong—in our lives and in our world—and to show us how to get in on God's project to make things better. Sometimes, conflict is a result. Sometimes "stirring" is required to bring about change. The Rev. Dr. Martin Luther King Jr. knew that many folks were uncomfortable with public, disruptive actions like sit-ins and marches. Writing from the Birmingham jail, he taught that discomfort was part of the point, saying that nonviolent public actions *seek* to "establish such creative tension that a community that has consistently refused to negotiate is forced to confront the issue. It seeks so to dramatize the issue that it can no longer be ignored."[7]

This is what we experience as communities rise up in peaceful protest, determined to dramatize the issues of police brutality and white supremacy so that these pervasive realities can no longer be ignored. Pride parades and demonstrations keep the call for justice for LGBTQ persons in front of those who would prefer to ignore or deny the injustice of the status quo. The marches that have flooded my hometown of Washington, DC, over the past months, the protests and rallies, all "disturb the peace," not for fun, but for the sake of love and the cause of right. The creative tension of these actions extends into conversations between friends and among families as persons choose where to stand. Perhaps "creative tension" is not how you would describe what you experience with some of your family and friends when it comes to difficult conversations. But one important aspect of faith is to prayerfully, thoughtfully, and humbly interpret the scriptures and the tradition, to choose where you will stand, and to risk creating conflict for what you believe to be loving and just.

When you speak and act from a place of thoughtful, humble, loving discernment, and, as a result, people challenge you, "unfriend" you on Facebook, treat you like you are ridiculous, naive, uninformed, or downright sinful for where you stand or for who you are, remember that you are in good company. The late, modern prophet Rev. William Sloane Coffin says, "Jesus knew that 'love your enemies' didn't mean 'don't make any.' "[8]

All of this is difficult for me. I know that one of my gifts/temptations is to be a "pleaser." I know how to discern and provide what people want. I am a master of "smooth talk." One of the roles I played in my family system was peacekeeper, anxiety manager, and protector. I have a learned allergy to anger and rage. None of this prepares me for the work of disturbing the peace for the sake of the Kin-dom. But walking closely with Jesus, knowing Spirit has my back, and trusting that God sees into my heart and holds me in love—that prepares me for whatever hard work I am given, even the hard work of disappointing people or "losing people" from my congregation or making someone really, really angry.

My guess is that no one thinks the world is as God would have it to be. Things need to change. Conflict is often required to make change happen. It is a risky place to stand, but the good news is that we can participate in God's activity in the world to make things different. Like Jesus, we are called to embody the ways of God's Kindom, to help usher it in, to make it real in the world, to challenge anything in the world that doesn't reflect God's love and justice. To "disturb the peace" will bring us into places of conflict. But it will also bring us into God's work for real peace—not the kind achieved by denial or burying ourselves in illusions, but the peace that comes through truth-telling and sacrificial love. And we are assured that God will give us grace to persevere, courage to stand on the side of justice and peace, a reward that is beyond anything we can imagine, and most certainly a reality better than the way we've always done it.

WHAT DO WE DO?

Let the beauty we love be what we do.

—Rumi

God has shown you, O mortal, what is good. And what does the Lord require of you?
To act justly and to love mercy and to walk humbly with your God. (Mic 6:8 NIV)

t is hard to be a Christian in America."[1] This simple statement of pastor Jonathan Wilson-Hartgrove haunts me. He writes, "Almost everywhere I go these days, people agree that something is wrong in American Christianity. Whether I'm talking to Pentecostals or Presbyterians, Democrats or Republicans, academics in a coffee shop or neighbors on their front porch, there seems to be a consensus on this: the church in America isn't living up to what it's supposed to be."[2] He goes on to say that the consensus quickly breaks as soon as he tries to get specific about what the problem is; fingers start to get pointed everywhere. He continues, "Unity across dividing lines was what distinguished the early church—so much so that they required a new name. Christianity was a new identity, neither Jew nor

Gentile, male nor female, slave nor free (Gal. 3:28)....It's hard for anybody in America to look at the first Christians and feel very proud about where we are now."[3] These words were written in 2008. Lord knows things have not improved. The divides are deeper and wider than ever; the Christian witness in the public square is—to use the present vernacular—a hot mess.

I want to make a clear distinction: it is not hard to *say* we are Christian in America—it's not like we have to hide our faith for fear of getting put on a "Christian registry" or out of fear for our lives or the lives of those we love. But if being Christian means living in a peculiar way that truly mirrors the life and teachings of Jesus as citizens of the Kin-dom, then being Christian in America is difficult. Kin-dom values and "American" values don't always line up. And we can't help but participate in systems of oppression, violence, and injustice as citizens of the United States.

That may seem like an overstatement. But ponder these questions:

- Do you purchase goods and services, some of which will be produced with child labor or in ways that pollute the earth or that don't pay workers a living wage?

- Do you pay taxes, some of which support policies that hurt the poor and pay for instruments of death?

- Do you avail yourself of any privilege you're afforded by way of your race, education, income, ability, gender identity, or sexual orientation—privileges woven into the fabric of American culture?

The life and teachings of Jesus would have something to say about all those things. We might debate the finer points of interpretation and application for our current realities. But, try as we might, we can't escape our complicity. It's hard to be Christian in America.

In the midst of so deep a collusion, what are we to do? How do we resist? One of the things I hear often is that there are too many challenges to address and resist. What difference can we possibly make, and where do we even begin? My response is this: all we can do is what we can do, and we can do something or we can do nothing. Either way, we're making a difference for better or worse.

There is a poem titled "Stubborn Ounces" that serves as a reminder of this for me. It uses the image of a "hovering scale" of justice, and our "little efforts" are added to one side or the other. The poet acknowledges those who think our small acts will make no difference in tipping the scale. But in the end, what is affirmed "beyond debate" is "my right to choose which side shall feel the stubborn ounces of my weight."[4]

Who and what feels "the stubborn ounces of [your] weight"? You change the world by engagement or disengagement. You have a right to choose. There is urgency about the decisions you make. But how to decide? How do we discern what to do, how to speak, and when to respond?

Discernment

I recently heard a John Wesley scholar assert a simple guideline for how to know when to resist: when what is happening is contrary to the love of neighbor. This is a good starting point, of course. It is biblical. It is straightforward. It is not overly complicated. There are those who would parse the word *love*. What one person believes is loving may be received as hurtful to another. However, the way I understand love is based on the revelation of God's love through Jesus of Nazareth. God loves the world. God desires life to flourish. God heeds the cries of the suffering and is always working for good in the world. God invites us to participate in caring for the life of the world and to be vigilant against all that threatens life. Jesus embodied the fullness of this love and desire—in his life on earth and in his death on the cross. From this, a slightly more fleshed-out version of the aforementioned guide for discerning when to engage in sacred resistance follows:

> Faithfulness to the crucified one means, *concretely* speaking, a primary identification with "the crucified people." . . . The consequence of this "cross-consciousness" is the creation in the "body of Christ," of a vigilance for oppression and injustice. . . . Not always, but normally, the confession of the faith arises just at the point at which Christian watchfulness recognizes that the powerful of the world have gone too far. . . . When the powerless are victimized—whether this means powerless people or powerless creatures of any sort, and whether this means physical victimization or more subtle types of oppression—then the faithful church resists.[5]

My shorthand categories for ethical discernment based on these biblical and theological convictions are: What is life-giving/nurturing/promoting? What is death-dealing, life-destructive, life-taking? Life and death. This is what is at stake in our discernment. Using our best energies and the spiritual and rational tools at our disposal (scripture, tradition, experience of God, and reason), we are called to discern if something is life-giving or death-dealing. And then we have to decide how to respond.

Staying Informed

In addition to biblical study and reflection upon the theological and ecclesiastical traditions of our faith, an important part of discernment is paying attention—staying awake and alert to what is happening in our communities and our world. We live in a world that is inundated with news, data, blogs, tweets, posts, articles, essays, reports, briefs, and information to the point that it can feel suffocating and become difficult to choose where to look or whose voice to heed. We've also entered a strange era in which "fake news" is not only found in *Saturday Night Live* skits but also proffered through media outlets that present themselves as legitimate sources. The old quip "don't confuse me with the facts" has become less of a joke and more of a demand. In this deeply chaotic, confusing, and overwhelming context, how do we stay awake and informed without losing our sanity?

In the months following the 2016 presidential election, I heard all sorts of perspectives on this topic. Some folks said we needed to be more vigilant than ever in staying informed and up to date on what is happening. Others said the thing to do is turn the news off completely because it's simply too damaging, too full of "spin," and ultimately not helpful. Still others were working on strategies to hover between the "all-in" or "cut it off" extremes—and sought out a measured, balanced diet of solid journalism from several different perspectives. Many folks have no choice about whether or not to follow the news because their jobs require knowledge of the headlines and engagement in the conversation. But even if that's not your reality, for those of us committed to sacred resistance, it is important to find ways to stay informed.

My dad taught me that when you find yourself facing a challenge, the first thing to do is assess what resources you have and what you can actually *do* to make any kind of helpful response. In this case, what we *can't* do is inform or change anyone else. We are called to inform ourselves to the very best of our ability—even in the midst of all the chaos.

As I've pondered this, I became aware of the psychological and sociological research on something called "confirmation bias." What is confirmation bias? One article lays it out in terms of our misconception and the truth:

- The Misconception: Your opinions are the result of years of rational, objective analysis.

- The Truth: Your opinions are the result of years of paying attention to information which confirmed what you believed while ignoring information which challenged your preconceived notions.[6]

The author shares a number of studies and experiments on confirmation bias, including one on Amazon purchasing trends during the 2008 US presidential election. This study reveals that Obama supporters purchased books that praised him—and those who didn't support him bought books that didn't praise him! In other words, folks purchased the books not for new information but for confirmation of their previously held views. For more than fifty years, studies have consistently shown that confirmation bias is a stumbling block across contexts. For example, journalists may be tempted to avoid or ignore data that would challenge the story they want to tell; and researchers may struggle to design experiments that leave much room for any outcome but the one they desire.[7]

Studies suggest that we remember things that support our beliefs and forget what doesn't. And there's also something referred to as the "makes sense stopping rule" in which we come up with an answer then work to prove it right instead of testing to see if it is wrong. When we find an answer to a question that seems to make sense based on our existing presumptions, we stop looking for answers.

The lure of confirmation bias may best be confirmed by the loyalty and passion directed toward various pundits in the mainstream media. Pundits of all political stripes are like gasoline on a fire, providing big doses of filtered language to fuel existing perspectives.

> Whether or not pundits are telling the truth, or vetting their opinions, or thoroughly researching their topics is all beside the point. You watch them not for information, but for confirmation.... Over

time, by never seeking the antithetical,... you can become so confident in your world-view no one could dissuade you.[8]

Before a few months ago, I didn't know the term "confirmation bias" but was certainly familiar with the concept of speaking in an "echo chamber" or "living in a bubble." So, as I read about confirmation bias, I wasn't surprised—except for how deeply convicted I felt. After all, just because I don't listen to the likes of Rush Limbaugh doesn't mean that I willingly ignore *all* information that counters my preconceptions, right? I want to believe that my perspectives and stances are rational and tested against the objective resources of scripture, science, and so on. But how have I fallen prey to this tendency to block anything that might truly challenge my worldview? If I— and we—seriously value real listening, discernment, and facts and want to engage in the self-examination required to engage in sacred resistance faithfully, we need to wrestle with this. After all, confirmation bias is driven by our desire to be "right"; but God wants us to be faithful—to be loving, wise, humble, and just.

We can't do anything about how confirmation bias has formed or affected us up until today and likely can't wrest ourselves of this tendency completely even once we acknowledge its existence. But, as with any life-limiting practice, the first step toward freedom is admitting we have a problem. We can at least *try* to resist living in the illusion that "our opinions are the result of years of rational, objective analysis" (and that anyone who disagrees with us is deluded or "evil"). For example, as we wrestle with the challenging issues of our day—things like immigration, Israel-Palestine, poverty, abortion— we can acknowledge those aspects of our position that may be (if we're honest) little better than convenient rationalizations. To counter the effects of confirmation bias doesn't require me to start regularly watching news programs that make me anxious and angry. But perhaps it does mean that I need to intentionally look for and seek to understand (nonsensationalized) perspectives that are truly counter to my own. The goal is not to be converted to some other position necessarily but rather to be truly open to the experience and perspective of another person or group, to allow myself to be truly challenged.

We cannot make anyone else willing to be open to *our* experience and perspective. All we have control over is what *we* are willing to do. And by the grace of God we will listen to, seek to understand, learn from, and have compassion for those whose paths and positions and politics challenge our own.[9]

Overcoming Fear

Fears and doubts too long have bound us;
free our hearts to work and praise.
Grant us wisdom, grant us courage, for the living of these days.

—*Harry Emerson Fosdick, "God of Grace and God of Glory"*

Somewhere I saw Stanley Hauerwas quoted as saying, "It's hard to remember that Jesus did not come to make us safe, but rather to make us disciples." I don't have the exact reference for this but, from what I know of Hauerwas, it sounds like him. Following Jesus is not for the faint of heart. And, at the same time, "the faint of heart"— those who are fearful and lack courage—are among those most in need of Jesus. In Jesus we meet the grace, strength, friendship, and perfect love of God. And, as it is written in 1 John 4:18, "perfect love casts out fear." If God loves us, if God is "for us," what do we have to fear? If God is for us, who is against us (Rom 8:31)? As we allow ourselves to comprehend the power of God's steadfast love, that love will set us free from so much that binds us, from messages, manipulations, and illusions that leave us stuck in lives smaller than the lives we're made for. In Jesus we see God's love fuel courage to face the worst the world can do, strength to love enemies, and triumph over death itself.

God's love is indeed powerful and can set us free to live more fully and with greater courage. But as one of my spiritual guides likes to remind me, "There's no safety in being free."

To follow Jesus means that personal safety is not our first priority. Instead, the priority is receiving and sharing the love of God. The priority is to become more like Christ. That will mean facing our personal fears and the obstacles to living with an open heart. It will mean overcoming inner anxieties about living with open hands and open arms. So much in human experience and the brokenness of human relationship teaches us to be guarded and afraid, to clutch and seek to control. To learn how to be yourself and to share yourself generously, to "risk your significance,"[10] is part of the curriculum for Christian discipleship. It is the work of our lifetime. It is a daily practice. As we continue on the journey of this love-fueled freedom, Christ's call will find expression in our lives in some form or fashion. Jesus used the words of Isaiah to describe his call: to bring good news for the poor, release for the captives, new vision for those in darkness, and freedom for the oppressed (Luke 4:18).

Throughout the Bible, those called to follow God are often afraid and painfully aware of their frailties and shortcomings. It's OK to be honest about our fear. We wouldn't be human if we didn't feel the fear that rises up when threatened with physical harm or the loss of things we hold dear. Even Jesus prayed that the cup of suffering might pass from him (Matt 26:39). But those who engage in sacred resistance, seeking to embody the love of God and to become more like Christ, will put themselves in places of risk and danger for the sake of the call to love, peace, and justice.

Having said this, it is important to be discerning about how and when to knowingly put yourself in harm's way. There will be times when a public action will have the potential for violence or arrest. There will be times when something you write will have the potential for misunderstanding and attack. There will be moments when your alignment with a movement or solidarity with people will have the potential for loss of collegial support, friends, or even family relationships. Pastors know that taking a stand in word or deed on a controversial issue may not only result in the loss of beloved church members and much-needed revenue but might also result in the loss of their livelihood, their job. There are choices to be made in these and all risky situations. Only you—in prayer and reflection—can weigh the promise of an action against its possible costs in your life and context. One of the clarifying questions I often ask myself: if my name were ever to appear in the recorded history of the years during which I sojourned on this planet, what is the story of my life I would be proud to have told?

A haunting and clarifying word is that of Martin Luther King Jr., who is often credited with saying, "Our life begins to end the moment we become silent about things that matter." It is confirmed for me over and again: life and death are at the heart of all our discerning.

And a critical practice of discernment is listening, not only to scripture and through prayer but also to the wisdom and experience of others. Do seek out counsel from trusted companions on your journey. You are never alone. Even in moments when friends may seem remote, hold fast to the promise that God will never leave nor forsake you. Our God is with you to guide and encourage:

Do not fear, for I have redeemed you;
    I have called you by name, you are mine.
When you pass through the waters, I will be with you;
    and through the rivers, they shall not overwhelm you;
when you walk through fire you shall not be burned,

and the flame shall not consume you.
Do not fear, for I am with you. (Isa 43:1b-2, 5a)

What Do We Do?

I have suggested a variety of ways to ground our lives in such a way that we embody sacred resistance. First and foremost, we do this through participation in communities of faith that trust God's wisdom and way for life together and whose engagement in the world seeks to be visible as a real alternative. Living life for and with others in study, prayer, sacrament, relationships of mutual care and respect, deep listening and humility; seeing the human face in every "issue"; keeping crisis in perspective; practicing love and nonviolence; and seeking the common good—all of these are concrete practices of sacred resistance. These are things we can do.

Here I endeavor to address several other concrete ways to mobilize sacred resistance in moments of acute challenge and concern. The shape of what follows is inspired by theologian Douglas John Hall's reflections upon the Christian *confession* as word, deed, and stance.[11]

Word

There have been times in worship when the pastor or worship leader says something I may have heard or thought or believed as simple fact (for example, "black lives matter."). But when the words are spoken aloud in the context of faith community, in sacred space, it feels like they press against some deep place in me and in the space between and among those gathered. The spoken word has power.

Sometimes, after another tragedy or travesty emerges in the daily news, I forget that it is important to say something—it's important because *not* saying something says something. We need to speak the words—even if they have been said before, even if we think those who hear the words already know or believe them, even if it feels tiresome to have to keep repeating them, even when many others are saying them, too. We need to speak the words as directly as we can, as lovingly as we can, as clearly as we can.

- The words we need to speak are words of God's love, mercy, justice, hope, and promise.

- The words we need to speak are words that connect God's resistance to our own.

- The words we need to speak are words that name the pain we experience and see in and around us.

- The words we need to speak are words that unmask injustice.

- The words we need to speak are words that describe both how we can love God and love others and the ways we are failing to uphold that commandment.

- The words we need to speak are words that give shape to our hope.

- The words we need to speak are words that acknowledge that the church is both aware and concerned about the things that people are dealing with every day, the things that are in the news, the things that are causing distress, the things that are confusing and overwhelming in the world.

I have already acknowledged—without sufficiently illuminating—the ways that scripture and theology, the *words* of our faith, get interpreted and applied in polar-opposite ways. Words can be twisted and parsed and used for very targeted purposes. Words can, in fact, be "weaponized." Words can also be made impotent, stripped of their teeth. Whether with good or malicious intent, words are malleable. This is why it is of critical importance that we give thought to our words and that they be grounded in a "meditative core"[12]—that is, in the peculiar story and way of God revealed in the scriptural tradition of our faith. This "meditative core" allows us to stand within the culture and still engage it from the perspective of the Kin-dom of God. Only from that place will we be able to counter the fact that "churches in North America tend to *reflect* rather than to *engage* our society" and that "this is as much the case with the liberal and 'radical' elements in the churches as it is with most conservative groupings."[13]

In response to the fact that folk will continue to claim that they are basing their words and actions on scripture and the broader tradition while landing in radically different places, I agree that

all that responsible theological thought may say on the matter is contained in the test that Jesus, according to the record, articulated: "You will know them by their fruits" (Mt 7:16). If anyone can demonstrate to the community of faith, on the grounds of Scripture and tradition that the so-called "German Christians" who took up with enthusiasm Hitler's racial and other policies were acting as faithful disciples of the Jewish man whom faith confesses to be the Christ, I shall be astonished.[14]

We cannot control what others will say or how they will speak. Our responsibility is to give thought and care for our own words— the words we use in interpersonal relationships as well as the official words of our churches (or synagogues or mosques). Congregational words are shared—or can be—in a variety of ways: preaching, teaching, and open "letters" or statements on issues or in response to events. What follows are some thoughts on each of these "official" ways of speaking the faith.

Preaching

"I went to worship this morning and not one word was spoken about [fill in the blank]." I've heard this again and again from folks who, in the wake of a significant moment in our nation or world, went to worship hoping for a word to provide some spiritual framework within which to hold grief, outrage, shock, or pain. Instead, they experienced faith communities who, intentionally or not, communicated disconnection from what was weighing upon the minds and hearts of many in the congregation. It's true that some who come to worship may want to avoid difficult topics in church—out of fear, conflict-aversion, exhaustion, or any number of other reasons. People are dealing with difficult things every day. It is important for preaching to speak to the perennial, human challenges of relationships, illness, trust, faith, and the like. But there are moments when scripture and the pastoral and ethical teachings of our tradition could offer powerful resources for people trying to figure out how to feel and what to do in response to something that is happening in their city, nation, or world. There will always be people who insist that "politics don't belong in church." In response, these words express my deeply held conviction:

> To stand apart from the complex and often morally corrupt world of political involvement and responsibility in the name of Jesus Christ is to dishonor that name—the name of one who was hauled before the authorities precisely because his "saving work" was perceived to be (and really was!) political.[15]

If the church is to participate in God's ongoing creative work of love, compassion, mending, and making new, and to prepare persons to be ready in moments of crisis to discern where and how God is calling them to respond, then there are instances when the preacher needs to speak up—whether everyone wants to hear it or not.

In my experience, even in the most socially and politically engaged congregations, there are some who will react against sermons that address current events or social issues. Every preacher I know agrees that even sermons about seemingly innocuous topics can be heard in ways that offend or upset some in the congregation. Preaching is risky business. We who are called to this vocation put ourselves on the line every time. We have to choose how to read the scripture, how to interpret it, how to connect it to human life in our context, and then we have to *say something*. There will inevitably be opportunities missed or connections we struggle to help people make. But our spiritual tradition has something to say, has words that speak to the pain, injustice, confusion, and chaos of our day. It is up to preachers to speak the words.

I've been asked a lot lately how to preach on controversial, politically charged topics. The first response I share is that, if you are a pastor, the relationship with your congregation is the place to begin. If the people trust that you see, know, and love them, that you love God and seek God's wisdom and way in your speaking and choosing, and that you are on a journey with God and with them in relationship, you have a good foundation to stand upon. From such a place of trusting relationship, preachers can risk taking a stand—or can at least share where they find themselves at any given moment.

Many years ago, when I preached a sermon that addressed violence, weapons, and the military, a member of my congregation who was serving in the military said, "I almost walked out during your sermon today because I felt offended and angry. But then I realized that you were trying to think these things through and so I decided to stay." This parishioner was one I regularly struggled to understand, even as we became friends. Our lives and ways of seeing and processing the world are radically different. But in that community, we shared ministry and respected each other. Our relationship allowed her to be angry, to disagree, and to keep trying to listen even when she would have been more comfortable to just leave.

We don't always have interpersonal relationships with all who hear our sermons. And, in a context of radical polarization, even close relationships may not be able to withstand the temptations to reactivity (fight or flight) born by "trigger" words or inflammatory topics. Pastor Tom Berlin provides helpful, practical guidance for preaching in a politically polarized congregation.[16] He advises that the preacher begin with humility, do enough research that the sermon is informative and interesting on the topic (not just warmed-over platitudes), and be thoughtful and fair with regard to the variety of perspectives on the topic. Rev. Berlin writes:

> I find it helpful to state my opinion on the sermon topic and share how scripture informs my thinking. This is the shortest part of the sermon. My desire isn't to convince others but to model the vulnerability necessary for people with differing perspectives to live in Christian community. It's amazing how much more latitude people will give you if they trust that you're honest about your opinion and fair to theirs.[17]

I'm not sure I do this very well myself on a regular basis. It's very good counsel and reminds me to try to invite the congregation to think things through with me. Recently, again in a sermon on violence, I began with these words:

> I've been dreading preaching this sermon for a long time. It is a sermon about what Jesus teaches about violence. It is a sermon about the ways that violence is one of the favored idols in American culture. It is a sermon that challenges our assumptions about what creates, maintains, and assures our security. It is a sermon that is impossible to preach without leaving out important context, history, and nuance. It's a sermon that raises more questions than answers. It's a sermon that's impossible to preach without stepping on everyone's toes; it's an "equal aggravation" kind of message. In fact,

in my preparation, I have found myself profoundly convicted and uncomfortable. But this sermon is important; because it names an often unspoken but constant and pervasive challenge to those of us who try to follow Jesus. And it's appropriate we acknowledge this challenge now, through these weeks of Lent, as we seek to identify places where our hearts and lives are not fully aligned with the way of Jesus, the way of life in God's Kin-dom.

This was my attempt at extending an invitation for folks to grapple with difficult stuff and to hear that I, as the preacher, was also grappling. A comment I received that day: "I hated hearing that sermon as much as you hated having to preach it. It's really hard stuff." Being honest and invitational in the midst of difficult topics won't allow everyone to hear you, but it certainly doesn't hurt.

In times of relative peace, preachers can speak words that help raise the consciousness of the congregation about ongoing issues— things like poverty, the cradle to prison pipeline, rampant materialism, homelessness, climate change, and so on. And in times of crisis, preachers have a responsibility at least to try to offer an interpretive, pastoral, and energizing word to their congregation that provides encouragement and guidance from the biblical and theological tradition, a word that reminds folks of what it means to live as citizens of God's Kin-dom within the day-to-day challenges of life in this world.

When I struggle with what to say, turning back toward the scriptural text gives me what is needed. When in doubt, preach the text! One of my favorite lines is, "I'm not making this up. It's in the book!" I'm not suggesting looking for so-called proof-texts that will simply prop up your political or moral position. Rather, you might draw upon the Revised Common Lectionary or some other cycle of readings so that you are challenged to preach on a text not of your own choosing. When I do this, it always surprises me the resonance to be found with what is happening in the world. Regardless of how you choose the text, there is something powerful about a close, deep reading and exposition of a biblical story or passage. What I've found is that such a reading will challenge people on all sides of any issue, and it has the potential to provide powerful guidance and comfort as well. I give thanks for a holy and living word that has so much to say to us in every age.

Pastoral Letters and Congregational Statements

Pastors reading this book will know that there are a variety of things that need to be addressed in the preaching of a congregation. We are trying to teach spiritual practices, create loving and intentional communities, inspire greater generosity and shared ministry, and much more. As one colleague said to me recently, "I can't rewrite every sermon based on the latest crisis in the news!" Discerning when to pivot from the plan and write a new sermon based on something that has happened is an ongoing challenge. We have to listen carefully to our hearts and to watch for the Spirit's leading in prayer. When the culminating sermon for an important preaching series coincides with a national tragedy, what is to be done? There may be a way to work both topics into the preaching moment. But it may require too much verbal acrobatics and feel forced to do so.

As an alternative, it can be very powerful to draft a letter or statement to be read aloud during worship that addresses the tragedy or event that needs to be lifted up. These statements generally need to be drafted quickly—sometimes within a window of only hours. Having a process in place is helpful. In churches with larger clergy teams, appoint one person to write a draft and then circulate to the team for comment and edits. All clergy can sign, and the statement can be shared as a pastoral letter. In smaller churches, the same kind of process can be engaged among the pastor and key lay leadership. It is particularly powerful for this kind of letter or statement to come from more than one person—the clergy team, clergy and governing body, or key lay leadership. Reading the statement aloud in worship and then following the reading with prayers is a simple and faithful way of speaking directly to the situation at hand.

Some congregations will have, in addition to scripture, denominational or congregational "core values," social principles, or other broader statements that provide guidance for the response to any given situation. It is important for public statements to draw upon such resources and to represent the community with integrity. Even when this is done with care, not everyone in a congregation will fully support every public statement or stance. For this reason, it is particularly important for the statement to find its grounding in scripture and other shared statements and commitments.

Depending upon your context, the letter or statement may be distributed beyond worship on your website, via e-mail and "snail mail," on social media, and in the form of a press release.

Sometimes, it may be that both a sermon and a statement on the same crisis are appropriately included in worship. Again, this is a work of discernment for the preacher and congregational leadership. The critical piece is that the words get spoken one way or the other.

Teaching

In seasons of chaos and confusion, it is important to create space for folks to think, to learn, to be stretched, and to share their questions and perspectives with others. When words get spoken in a sermon or public congregational statement that highlight a particular challenge, injustice, or need, a follow-up opportunity for study and conversation can be not only helpful but also transforming. Consciousness-raising cannot fully take root in worship. Encourage book groups; lead forums on critical topics; invite scholars, activists, trainers, and organizers to your church. Look for opportunities in your community or networks to share with your congregation.

A few recent examples from the congregation I serve:

- a Saturday workshop led by Cook-Ross (CookRoss.com) on developing intercultural competency

- rapid-response trainings in support of vulnerable immigrant populations

- annual scholar in residence program consisting of three to four lectures/workshops per year; annual topics include racial justice and engaging in political conversation and civil public discourse

- annual Advent social justice series consisting of weekly forums with guest presenters on questions and issues related to the congregation's missional priorities and strategy

- book studies on a variety of topics

It can feel overwhelming to think about all the topics that merit attention. Discernment is key. Regardless of the size of your faith community, it is important to identify where the needs in the community and the passion of your people connect. If there is a need to mobilize support for a particular cause in your community, preach, teach, and then coordinate actions in concert to create the "on-ramps" for people to engage. It may be that the congregational priorities limit the number of topics you can engage programmatically at any given time. However, it is possible to provide resources for further study or exploration by way of book lists, referrals to trainings, retreats, advocacy organizations, and more.

In the kind of days we're living, it is as important as ever for the church to provide solid scholarship and opportunities to engage in deep dialogue about the critical issues we're facing as a society and world. The more congregations provide resources and encourage study and dialogue, the broader the reach of a meaningful and transforming word.

Deed

At the beginning of this book, I provide contours of a vision for sacred resistance. I suggest that our deeds:

- counter the forces of hatred, cruelty, selfishness, greed, dehumanization, desolation, and disintegration in God's beloved world;

- rely on biblically and relationally grounded faith to discern how to be actively engaged with the world;

- take shape publicly in how we live our lives in community;

- extend publicly through acts including communal protest, political advocacy, and risky solidarity;

- be contextual and inspired by a radically free God who calls us to cross boundaries to share and care for life with and for others.

As with the decisions related to when and what to speak, choosing when and how to actively engage in the public square requires intentional discernment. I've emphasized study, engaged communal life, staying informed, guarding against confirmation bias, and prayer as tools for discernment. If you are discerning whether to take a personal action, whether to attend a rally or march, to sign a petition or open letter for example, these tools will be very important and helpful to self-monitor your motives, your integrity, your tolerance for risk, your level of commitment, and your hope.

The same is true for discerning acts to be engaged by churches or faith communities. However, in addition, there are some other considerations that come into play in community. Not only will it be important to ground actions in more than a proof-text of scripture and the core values or mission of the congregation, but also it will be imperative to consider the implications of any action for the community over the long haul.

Some acts will be clearly consistent with the gospel and therefore not that complicated. Though, I hasten to add, even signing a letter can lead to questions or controversy based on who else "signs on." Other kinds of action may seem straightforward but can also invite concern and consternation. When Foundry's Sacred Resistance ministry promoted participation in the Women's March in January 2017, I had more than one conversation with parishioners about the "messiness" and unpredictability of such an event. One conversation went like this: "I understand that Foundry believes this is an important event to promote based on a number of social justice issues. But I'm concerned that it may turn into primarily a rally about abortion and I'm deeply conflicted about that." This person wanted to support Foundry and our collective commitments and was discerning whether she could do that with integrity. In response, the best I could do was share that our Sacred Resistance Ministry Team had discerned that the stated values and mission of the Women's March were in line with Foundry's values and mission. But that there was no way to know or to control all the messages that would "show up" at such a large grassroots event. I said to my parishioner, "We have to weigh the primary message and goal and determine whether the risk is worth it. In this case, even though it will certainly be messy, Foundry believes we need to show up."

As I said about preaching, choosing where to show up, how to lend our name, and what to support is risky. I have argued in an earlier chapter that an intentionally Kin-dom-aligned, cross-shaped community will be more prepared to mobilize timely action with clarity and conviction. And for that or any community, it will be important to consider some of the following questions and concerns.

Where do the resources and passion of our congregation connect with the concrete needs in the larger community?

When there are so many causes, crises, and critical needs that press for our response, a clarifying piece of discernment is to identify which needs connect most with your congregation's passion and resources. No congregation can attend to everything. Some churches may grow large enough that small groups and home groups begin to mobilize around particular areas of shared passion and/or expertise. But even for large faith communities, there needs to be focus and strategic prioritization in order for efforts to have the greatest effect. Here again it is helpful to remember that we participate in God's work of mending together with many others in the body of Christ and in the broader beloved community of God's family. Gifts and strengths abound.

Different congregations will have different strengths and passions. I have served congregations who had human resources for brick-and-mortar building, repair, and contracting. I have served congregations with passion and skill for policy critique, development, and legislative strategy. I have served congregations who had human resources for direct service with the poor and vulnerable through feeding, training, teaching, and so on. Some congregations will have resources across these and many other broad categories of ministry. What is important is to identify the gift(s) that your community of faith offers to the cause at hand. What can you offer that others may need?

This question helped give shape to Sacred Resistance Ministry at Foundry UMC. Foundry is located in the heart of the nation's capital and is made up of folks who care deeply about social justice and the common good. Many of those folks have skill and experience in advocacy, legislative process, politics, and communications. As I began to recognize how overwhelming things were going to be in the public square moving forward, I asked myself the question: What does Foundry have to contribute? How can we best serve the common good right now? The answer was this announcement in December 2016:

> In addition to all that Foundry already is and does, we are organizing to participate in sacred resistance of what appear to be real threats not only to the most vulnerable among us, but to all of us and to our planet. A team is convening to identify, vet, and publicize weekly actions of protest and resistance. We know there will be an ongoing need to engage and push back on proposed policies or actions; we also know there will be too much to keep track of on our own; we know that many opportunities will flash across our screens to engage—some which may have little (or dubious) impact. In response, the vision is to have a group of knowledgeable, committed folks be a kind of "clearing house" for actions that will have the greatest impact and that are of the highest priority at a given moment in time. With the weekly action shared on Sundays and through our website and social media, this will be a resource not only for those of us who are active in and through Foundry, but also for anyone who desires to stay awake and engaged in the work of prophecy. Many of you, through your vocational work or personal networks, will have information about things that need attention. We will share how you can suggest potential actions with the team.

I share this as one example of connecting a congregation's resources to the needs of the larger community. The Sacred Resistance Ministry Team continues to evolve as a resource not only for Foundry but also for others who can benefit from the insight and support of this group of faithful, committed disciples.

What is already happening in the community that our congregation can support?

It is sometimes tempting to think we need to create something new in order to meet a discerned need or to participate in sacred resistance. The truth is there are nonprofits, other faith communities, and grassroots movements likely already engaging in the work to which we are called. Even for the largest, most wealthy congregations, it makes sense and is deeply faithful to develop partnerships with other groups. Not only does this provide opportunities for listening and learning from other populations, but it also exponentially grows the network of engagement, expands the pool of resources and creativity, and offers the bonus of new relationships and companions for the journey.

What are the risks involved in our action, and how will we prepare for potential consequences?

Some actions and commitments will carry with them inherent risks. Congregations need to be honest and strategic in thinking this through. Increasingly, I hear about steps to take if arrested at a peaceful protest and regularly see images of people of faith and conscience being taken into custody for "disturbing the peace" or trespassing. We know there can be inherent risks of violence if we put our bodies in a place where grief, hatred, and rage are bubbling over. In addition to these kinds of risks, connected to public protests or actions, there are others to consider when looking at congregational stances or ongoing practices. Three examples immediately spring to mind from the context where I currently serve.

1. In a time before marriage equality was the law of the land (and before my arrival as pastor), Foundry found itself in a city that allowed legal marriage for all people and in a denomination that forbids its congregations and clergy

to perform same-gender marriages. The penalty for clergy can be trial and loss of credentials—and the loss of their job. The congregation engaged in a months-long season of discernment about its stance on Christian marriage, studying deeply, engaging in difficult conversations, and clearly addressing the benefits and risks in light of the church's long-standing commitment to LGBTQ equity, affirmation, and inclusion. The result was a decision by the congregation to practice marriage equality and to support any clergy who wished to perform marriages for same-gender couples. There was intentional thought given to strategy in the case of charges being filed. The congregation made a communal commitment to take this risk together for the sake of their calling.

2. After the shooting of Michael Brown in Ferguson, Missouri, Foundry began to have a series of conversations to discern a faithful response. Some in the congregation wanted to immediately hang a large banner emblazoned with #BlackLivesMatter outside the church building. In an intense moment during a workshop with the Rev. Dr. Alton Pollard, dean of Howard Divinity School, African American members expressed concern about hanging a banner without the engagement and commitment of the whole congregation. To publicly communicate a commitment to the Black Lives Matter movement without knowing the form our solidarity would take—actions, relationships, money, tangible support—smacked for many of an attempt to "check the box" and say we'd done our work on white supremacy without having to engage the same kind of deep work that had taken place around marriage equality. Dr. Pollard also made it quite clear that if the congregation chose to step out with such clear advocacy for racial equity and justice, there would be negative consequences. "Just get ready," he said. Stories abound not only of the defacement of signs and banners proclaiming Black Lives Matter but also of the ongoing violence against black and brown bodies

and those who stand with them. Foundry's intentional work of engagement and advocacy continues unabated. But at the time of this writing, there is no banner.

3. In the wake of the executive orders and other legislation affecting immigrants and ethnic minorities, our congregation began to grapple with the call to solidarity with vulnerable populations within the immigrant community. Our associate pastor for social justice brought this question to the board: "Are we willing to go to jail?" The point was that there were serious risks to the congregation, many of them unknown. What would happen if the congregation harbored those targeted by the US Immigration and Customs Enforcement (ICE) agency? What would happen to persons who accompanied immigrants to scheduled immigration appointments or intervened in an ICE raid? What were the legal protections, if any, for the congregation? For congregants who chose to offer shelter or solidarity in any form? Ultimately, we became founding members of the Sanctuary DMV (DC/Maryland/Virginia) movement, offering trainings for rapid response, supporting local nonprofits who provide legal and other assistance, and engaging in public advocacy for just and humane laws and policies for immigrants.

These are brief snippets to highlight the variety of issues to consider—denominational and livelihood risks, societal risks and risks to bodies and property, and legal risks.

There will be some risk any time we choose to step out and speak up to name oppression—our own or that of others. There will always be some risk when we choose to stand in solidarity with those whose lives and experience call out for justice and care. Congregations need to be honest and strategic in thinking through the risks so that the action and witness will have integrity, serve the common good, and provide the greatest possible support for those most in need.

Does the proposed action commit the congregation to ongoing engagement? If so, how will follow-through be assured?

While in a moment of outrage or grief, people mobilize and respond to calls to action, that initial burst of energy often dissolves, leaving a few people holding the proverbial bag of responsibility to carry the mission or movement forward. This cycle can cause disillusionment and be profoundly enervating for a community of faith. This isn't an issue with "one-off" actions in response to a discrete tragedy or injustice. But if the action makes a longer-term commitment (public affiliation as part of an ongoing coalition or movement, for example) thoughtful leaders will want to think through strategies and mobilize lay leadership to maintain meaningful engagement and accountability so that ongoing progress, needs, narratives, and challenges of the movement continue to fuel the congregation. Otherwise, the failure to follow through will be felt as just that—a failure—and no one is strengthened or energized by that.

What training or other resources are needed to equip leaders and members of the congregation to participate in the action?

This may seem obvious, but think about how to prepare for actions. When it is possible, seek the insight of others who have experience or expertise to share. You don't have to spend a year reading about an issue before acting, but it is important to think about resources and guidelines that will provide safety, grounding, and guidance for your folks.

I was moved by the witness of a colleague, then District Superintendent, now Bishop Cynthia Moore-Koikoi, who provided leadership for the United Methodist response in Baltimore immediately following the murder of Freddie Gray. A group of mostly clergy gathered in a church basement to organize for a witness in the streets of the Sandtown neighborhood the day after the unrest began. In the previous twenty-four hours, Bishop Moore-Koikoi had mobilized the movement of UMC clergy and laity, marched with an ecumenical group of Baltimore clergy (who'd subsequently been protected by both the Crips and Bloods in a rather unprecedented act of solidarity), and reached out to colleagues in Ferguson, Missouri, to ask for guidance. She said to the gathered body in the basement, "I knew we needed to be here, but I didn't know what I didn't know." Wise leaders will find the resources to fill in the gaps, to help us learn what we don't know so that our action will have the greatest possible impact.

A Prayer for the Journey

It is not easy to discern what to do. But we are called by God to do what we can. This famous prayer by Thomas Merton encourages me and, I hope, will offer you encouragement as well.

> *My Lord God, I have no idea where I am going.*
> *I do not see the road ahead of me.*
> *I cannot know for certain where it will end.*
> *Nor do I really know myself,*
> *and the fact that I think that I am following your will*
> *does not mean that I am actually doing so.*
> *But I believe that the desire to please you does in fact please you.*
> *And I hope I have that desire in all that I am doing.*
> *I hope that I will never do anything apart from that desire.*
> *And I know that if I do this you will lead me by the right road,*
> *though I may know nothing about it.*
> *Therefore will I trust you always,*
> *though I may seem to be lost and in the shadow of death.*
> *I will not fear, for you are ever with me,*
> *and you will never leave me to face my perils alone.*

Stance

"A picture paints a thousand words." I imagine this has always been true. It's not that words don't matter, but when what you say and how you *are* communicate different things, it's the way you are that will likely be remembered. Our associations with others and general way of being say a lot about who we are and what we value. If the church is understood as "a body," the position or "stance" of the body comprises what Douglas John Hall refers to as an "ecclesiastical body language."[18]

In moments of acute crisis or tragedy, therefore, an important consideration has to do with your "stance" as an individual or community of faith. This involves attention given to not only what action you take but also how you organize and with whom you choose to stand. What do people learn about you and your faith community simply through observation?

I recently experienced a situation in which I was involved with an emerging grassroots movement. Much energy went into the words that would try to capture the heart of the movement. Less robust attention was paid to questions of "stance." What do we look like? Who is lifted up in leadership? Are we as intentional about the "optics" as we are about the language? It's not that those involved in the movement didn't consider any of these questions; in truth, there was a good deal of conversation about the stance of the movement early on. But those considerations appeared lower on the priority list when it came time to invite others to engage. The reaction was predictable. The perceived stance of the new movement became an obstacle in communicating the vision.

The most straightforward guide for Christians when it comes to questions of "body language" is Jesus. A short list of elements of Jesus's stance:

- was born in obscurity to working-class parents who fled a

105

terror regime and became refugees (Luke 2; Matt 1–2)

- associates with the unorthodox movement of John the baptizer (Matt 3; Mark 1; Luke 3)

- refuses temptations of power, wealth, and fame (Luke 4; Matt 4)

- chooses ordinary people—some with bad reputations—to be his inner circle

- spends time with people considered unacceptable in polite society

- breaks religious rules to care for the marginalized, to engage in conversation and friendship with women, and to heal the sick

- enjoys being with children

Jesus seemed to be very intentional about where he stood, with whom he associated, for whom he would risk his safety. Jesus "took sides."

What side is Jesus on?

Two stories at the beginning of Jesus's public ministry provide insight. The first is the story of the devil tempting Jesus by saying, "If you are the Son of God then save yourself, worship me, do a sign." The devil promised a full belly, worldly power, and ego-stroking affirmation. Making this deal with the devil would have set Jesus on a certain kind of path (Luke 4:1-13). Instead, Jesus chose to worship God, to trust God, and to embark on a journey that would lead him not to fill his own belly but to feed the bodies and souls of the whole world; a journey that would set him against the powers of the world and that would inspire not ego-stroking affirmation but mocking and betrayal.

Immediately after that encounter in the wilderness, Jesus began teaching in the synagogues, eventually returning to Nazareth. He went into the synagogue on the Sabbath, as was his custom, and opened the scroll to the place where it was written,

"The Spirit of the Lord is upon me,
  because [God] has anointed me
  to bring good news to the poor.
[God] has sent me to proclaim release to the captives
  and recovery of sight to the blind,
  to let the oppressed go free,
to proclaim the year of the Lord's favor." (Luke 4:18-19)

Jesus says these verses of prophecy are fulfilled in him; in other words, this is his "position description." This is what it means for Jesus to side with God and not the devil: it means that Jesus sides with the poor, with the captives, with those who cannot see, with the oppressed. Jesus calls for fulfillment of the economic and social "reset" of a "jubilee" every fiftieth year—"the year of the Lord's favor"—when debts are canceled, tribal lands restored, and indentured servants set free.

Having claimed his role as God's anointed messenger and liberator, Jesus frames the message this way: "I must proclaim the good news of the kingdom of God . . . for I was sent for this purpose" (Luke 4:43). He describes the Kin-dom as that dynamic way of life-in-relationship that is characterized by the perfect love, the unity in diversity, the mutuality, the peace and justice of God's own triune life. To be a citizen of God's Kin-dom is to seek, by God's grace, to live in a way that reflects God's own love and life. The opposite to that way of life, a way we see manifest in some individuals and human communities and systems, is hateful, destructive, greedy, violent, and so on—what theologian Jon Sobrino calls the "anti-Kingdom." Novels and Hollywood provide ready examples of the struggle—think of Harry Potter's Professor Dumbledore and Lord Voldemort, *The Lord of the Rings'* Frodo and Sauron, Saruman, and their orcs, and (the now classic) Luke Skywalker and Darth Vader.

Jesus had to choose a stance and Jesus chose a side. It wasn't the side of the status quo. It wasn't the side of the strong and powerful. It wasn't the side of personal comfort or cheap grace. It wasn't the side of self-protection or revenge. It wasn't the side of wealth or privilege. Jesus chooses the underside, the outside, the pushed-aside. He stands on the side of justice, he stands on the side of self-giving love, and he stands on the side of humility and vulnerability. Jesus doesn't choose the side of the poor and oppressed because he loves only them. Jesus takes that side because he loves all people and knows that "when one part of the body suffers, the whole body suffers with it" (1 Cor 12:26, author's translation). As American Jewish poet Emma Lazarus wrote, "Until we are all free, we are none of us free." The only way we will ever all be free and whole is if we finally see one another, care for one another, sacrifice for one another, forgive one another, and love one another. This is what Jesus does. This is what Jesus chooses. And it leads to the cross. From that place of suffering, Jesus's "stance" remains consistent: solidarity with criminals, presence "outside the city"—beyond the boundaries of the center of worldly power—forgiveness for perpetrators of the anti-Kin-dom, and self-giving love and saving grace for all.[19]

Sacred resistance calls us to emulate Jesus's stance, to strive to be and become more like Christ. Are we able?

FUELING THE RESISTANCE: GUARDING AGAINST BURNOUT

Sacred resistance requires vigilance, energy, and patience. It demands hard work, sacrifice, and discernment. It can't happen without intentionality, discipline, and struggle. All this is, quite frankly, mentally, physically, and emotionally exhausting. We know that participation with God in the work of mending will continue throughout our lives—that its intensity and challenge will ebb and flow with the realities of a vulnerable, ever-changing world. It's "long haul" work, marathon work, and requires the kind of "pacing" that long-distance runners cultivate in order to be able to keep going.

What resources "keep our lamps fueled and burning" for the work of sacred resistance? In what follows I offer some things to consider as you seek to be realistic about the journey ahead and gracious with yourself and others as you travel.[1]

Remember the Sabbath

The apostles gathered around Jesus, and told him all that they had done and taught. He said to them, "Come away to a deserted place all by yourselves and rest a while." For many were coming and

> *going, and they had no leisure even to eat. And they went away in*
> *the boat to a deserted place by themselves. Now many saw them*
> *going and recognized them, and they hurried there on foot from all*
> *the towns and arrived ahead of them. As he went ashore, he saw*
> *a great crowd; and he had compassion for them, because they were*
> *like sheep without a shepherd; and he began to teach them many*
> *things. (Mark 6:30-34)*

"They had no leisure even to eat." Many of us can relate. There's just so much to do, demands at work, family needs and social calendars to manage, chores, bills, shopping, cleaning, not to mention our personal needs for exercise and personal growth. Then we place all this into the context in which we live—a world in which there are injustices to address, hungry people to feed, sick people to care for. There is violence and war and every other thing we encounter every day in the paper and on the news. And just for fun, throw in the personal events, crises, and issues that inevitably inhabit our lives—death, illness, unemployment, depression, relationship breakups and difficulties—and the positive things like new relationships, marriages, births, and new opportunities. Well, no wonder there's no time for leisure!

In the verses from Mark 6 above, Jesus's idea for a restful break never *really* gets off the ground. The overwhelming needs seem to meet the weary disciples at every turn. And Jesus—who never seems to suffer from compassion fatigue—had compassion for the suffering masses. If we only had this story to point to in order to reflect on Jesus's invitation to rest, we might conclude—if we are to follow Jesus—that we will never really take a break, that the overwhelming needs of our lives and of the world must always hold priority of place, and that we have to figure out some way not to get "compassion fatigue." But this is *not* the only instance we have in scripture of Jesus "stealing away." Earlier in Mark we hear that after a long evening of healing, Jesus got up early "in the morning, while it was still very dark...and went out to a deserted place, and there he prayed. And Simon and his companions hunted for him. When they found him, they said to him, 'Everyone is searching for you'" (Mark 1:35-37). We also have the story of Jesus who, after feeding the multitude, gave himself a time-out: "He made his disciples get into the boat and go on ahead to the other side, to Bethsaida, while he dismissed the crowd. After saying farewell to them, he went up on the mountain to pray. When evening came, the boat was out on the sea, and he was alone on the land. When he saw that they were straining at the oars against an adverse wind, he came towards them early in the morning, walking on the sea" (Mark 6:45-48).

Taken together, these passages show us that Jesus was determined to have time alone, time with God, time apart from the demands of his life—no matter how difficult or important the things were that were happening around him. Jesus was determined to make space for God, for rest, for prayer, regardless of the fact that "everyone was searching" for him, regardless of the "adverse winds" that were whipping up all around.

So where does all this leave us? The issue here is the spiritual practice of Sabbath. In Exodus 20:8-11 we find, "Remember the sabbath day, and keep it holy. Six days you shall labor and do all your work. But the seventh day is a sabbath to the LORD your God; you shall not do any work...in six days the LORD made heaven and earth, the sea, and all that is in them, but rested the seventh day; therefore the LORD blessed the Sabbath day and consecrated it." It seems that we take so seriously many of the other ten commandments, but with very little concern we blow off Sabbath rest. What's up with that?

Well, first of all, I think of the disciples saying to Jesus: "Everyone is searching for you." These days, Jesus would have an iPhone! No matter where Jesus was, he would be available; people wouldn't have to search for him. That's certainly the case for us. Our constant connection has many positive benefits, but it can also rob us of any real time, any breathing room. People can find us anywhere. We're never out of touch, always available. And we've come to believe that *this is as it should be.* God forbid that our connection gets lost—that we don't have reception! I must admit that the temptation here is very great—the temptation to make ourselves constantly available, to believe that we are indispensable. We tend to get caught up in this fiction that if we take a break—a real break—in which our phones, e-mail, and all the other connections are turned off (or not checked obsessively), then something terrible will happen: the world will stop turning; all our work will be lost; everything will fall apart. I want to gently suggest: this is not true.

The spiritual issue at play here is trust—trust that your work will not disappear if you take a break; trust that there are others who can manage in your absence; and, ultimately, trust that God is God and you're not. This is the biggie, of course. But if Jesus—Jesus of all people!—knew that it was important to go away and rest, then who are we to think that the world will fall apart if we do? You don't always have to be available. In fact, it is a good spiritual practice to intentionally make yourself *unavailable* in order to take a break and rest. When we haven't had a real chunk of downtime for awhile, all the needs and demands of our lives—no matter how valid—become occasions for resentment and short tempers.

Many folks will already be convinced that a restful break is not only important but also necessary. The trick comes in trying to make it part of our lives. The invitation/commandment is to do your work in six days and to practice Sabbath on the seventh; I highly recommend this. But it may be impossible for you to have a whole day set apart from work each week or to practice Sabbath in the midst of acute crises in which you are providing leadership or service. Thankfully, there is not a one-model-fits-all approach for incorporating Sabbath time into your life. I remember helping one guy figure out how he could claim Sabbath time as a student who also had a job.

He needed to work on Saturday morning and to pick up work again on Sunday afternoon; so he set the intention of making his Sabbath from noon Saturday to after church on Sunday. Sabbath time can also be folded into your daily or monthly as well as your weekly rhythm. But, like any spiritual practice, it requires intention and discipline.

Some of you may be wondering what it means to "practice Sabbath." What do you *do*? The biblical example calls us to lay down our work, to stop producing things, to let the field of our lives lie fallow for a time, to delight in the good work we have been so busy doing, to enjoy the fruits of our labors and of our lives. Sabbath practice is about doing things that renew and refresh, that energize and restore us, body and soul. Again, there is not a one-model-fits-all list of Sabbath practices, because different things will work for different people. Some may need to be alone while some may need time in relationship; some may need to be active and others might need to take a long nap; some may be renewed in the garden while others will need an urban dance party; sometimes time with the kids will be restoring and other times there may be a need for time apart.

In the midst of all this diversity of Sabbath practice, there is one thing that is true for us all: part of our "downtime" needs to be intentionally spent with God in prayer. Jesus "went away to a deserted place to pray." This is an important message for us to hear. Without going into a whole conversation about prayer, let me just say that the point is spending time with God, making space for God. If we really believe that God is the source of life, the wellspring of creativity and passion and peace, we'll make it a point to go back to that source again and again. How do you think Jesus was able to have constant compassion in the face of overwhelming need and conflict? He consistently and constantly spent time with God getting recharged for a life of service and love.

Weekly worship may be part of your Sabbath practice. Maybe you can incorporate even ten minutes each day to spend in prayer, to just make some space for God. And you don't always have to turn off your devices to spend time with God. For example, there's an app called "Pray as you go" that provides scripture and prayer and music reflection all done in ten to fifteen minutes. Ask friends about what online resources they find helpful in their spiritual practice. My guess is that you'll discover a variety of options for devotion and prayer that are as close as your cellphone.

In Jesus's invitation to "come away and rest awhile" we're given permission to stop doing things, to stop striving, and to just *be*. My paternal grandparents modeled a wonderful, balanced rhythm of doing and being in their lives. They lived in the Ozark hills of Arkansas and worked the land and lived pretty sustainably. They worked hard all day. And then, at the close of the day they engaged in a time-honored practice in that part of the world: porch-sitting. They would just rest, just be; they might visit with a neighbor who stopped by or with each other, or they might just watch the birds and the squirrels or the rain coming down. Other times, they might bring the dominoes out for a good time of play. They knew how to stop *doing* after a long day of work. We are given permission by no less than Jesus himself to come out to the porch and just *be*. Not forever—our responsibilities and the work of sacred resistance need our attention—but rather to establish a healthy rhythm of rest, renewal, and return.

"Laugh and Grow Strong"

There is a sculpture that has inspired and encouraged me for years. It has been in my pastor's study—often on my desk—since I received it as a gift from my mother. It has become a profound symbol for me of something deeply important in the spiritual life.

The sculpture is of a laughing pig. The pig is on its back, its two front hooves holding its round belly, mouth wide open in laughter. For me it's a sacred icon of earthy joy. I find it impossible to look at the giggling swine without feeling a shift in my spirit—a lightening up.

Laughter doesn't often get its due in Christian settings. In an attempt to be faithful, we can become awfully intense, we can take ourselves very seriously, and we can begin to feel responsible for every single problem and broken place in the world. That's a heavy load to carry. It's important to remember that we get to share in the work of new creation that God is always busy with, but we are not God! Lightening up doesn't mean we aren't taking our responsibilities seriously, but rather it means that we have proper perspective. That's good news if I've ever heard it; and I need to be reminded of this good news all the time. I need constant reminders to lighten up!

I have a running debate with a close friend about Jesus on this point. My friend tends to think that Jesus was too concerned with the great cosmic struggle between good and evil and the deeply bruising earthly struggle against greed and injustice to spend much time joking around or laughing. I, however, am convinced that all those children wouldn't want to be near Jesus if he didn't laugh and play. Everyone wanted Jesus to join their dinner parties; and he spent time with folks who knew how to have a good time. And, though in translation it's sometimes hard to recognize, some of Jesus's parables are deeply funny. All this is to say, I think Jesus laughed. A lot. And the more I learn about laughter, the more convinced I am of that.

Laughter is scientifically proven to have healing effects on our physical and mental health. It boosts our immune system, relieves muscle tension and stress, and causes the brain to release "endorphins, interferon-gamma (IFN), and serotonin. These are nature's own feel good chemicals and are responsible for helping to keep your mood uplifted."[2] Studies out of Harvard Medical School and the Mayo Clinic (among others) confirm that "nothing works faster or more dependably to bring your mind and body back into balance than a good laugh."[3] In other words, laughter is good medicine when you're stressed, ill, or discouraged.

I imagine all of us can think of a time when we were in the midst of a deep struggle or right in the middle of grief and found ourselves laughing with others; and in those moments we felt at least a moment of relief. There is deep folk wisdom in the phrase "sometimes you've got to laugh to keep from crying!"

In one study I consulted, I read that "laughter allows us to entertain the absurd and imagine alternate possibilities."[4] Laughter can bring relief to physical tension and stress, over-responsibility, disappointment, grief, taking ourselves too seriously, and lack of perspective. Christian writer and essayist Anne Lamott speaks to some of this saying:

> Humor and laughter and silliness and giggles can get into some dark, walled-off places inside us and bring breath and lightness....When I am at my most stressed, I sometimes lose my sense of humor, and that condition is just a nightmare....For me, hell is when I'm absolutely stuck in self-obsession, this terrible, terrible self-consciousness. The healing and grace often comes from being put back together by people... [who] somehow help me lighten up and get my sense of humor back. When I have my sense of humor back, nothing can stop me.[5]

Lamott describes humor and laughter as "carbonated holiness."[6] I love that way of thinking about the gift of laughter, as a bubbly, refreshing drink of God's grace, as the thing that is always available to us, just waiting to nourish and renew us body and soul: "A good laugh is a release—even if only for a moment—from worry, strife, and self. It is a sudden, often unbidden confession that someway, somehow, all is well, or at least there is a hope that it can be."[7]

I can't remember who wrote it, but someone once said that Christians should look more redeemed. That is, the good news of

God's ever-present love, mercy, and resurrection power should lead us to rejoice, to laugh and be glad! So, what are some ways that we can cultivate laughter in our lives? Here is a pretty good guide I found.[8]

Smile. Smiling is contagious! Practice smiling at anything and everything that is pleasant or kind. Try offering people a smile on the street instead of keeping your head down over your phone. Smile at the folks who serve you in a restaurant or at a service counter. Smile at your coworkers and family members. See what a difference all this smiling makes!

Count your blessings. Write them down. When you intentionally take stock of the positive things in your life, you guard against those depressing or upsetting thoughts that can get in the way of humor and laughter.

Spend time with fun, playful people. People who know how to laugh and be silly, who can see humor in the absurdities of life, and who have a playful disposition are good influences. Find them and let them influence you!

There are so many other ways to imbibe carbonated holiness:

- Watch a funny movie, TV show, or YouTube video
- Invite friends or coworkers to go to a comedy club
- Read the funny pages
- Share a good joke or a funny story
- Check out your bookstore's humor section
- Host game night with friends
- Play with a pet
- Goof around with children
- Do something silly
- Make time for fun activities (e.g., bowling, miniature golfing, karaoke)[9]

The practice is to intentionally seek out laughter in your life so that it becomes part of your regular spiritual diet, nourishing you for the long haul attending to the serious work of sacred resistance. Drink in the "carbonated holiness" that can refresh and renew! St. Ignatius, founder of the Jesuit order, once remarked to a novice, "I see you are always laughing, and I am glad of it." Ignatius also "once danced a jig to cheer up downcast Jesuits. He was a man whose joy was known to be full." So much so that the phrase "Laugh and grow strong" is often attributed to him.[10] Laugh and grow strong! Imbibe some carbonated holiness. Find *your* laughing pig and keep it ever before you!

Notice the Way the World Is

The way the world is can feel so heavy and leave us weary and hungry for something that nourishes our need for hope, for a sense of solid ground, for beauty, for tenderness. It was a gift and surprise to see that Pope Francis had done a TED talk[11] in which he speaks of our need for one another, of the need for a robust understanding and practice of solidarity, and for a "revolution of tenderness." What is the tenderness he talks about? "Tenderness is not weakness," he says, "it is fortitude":

> It is the love that comes close and becomes real. It is a movement that starts from our heart and reaches the eyes, the ears and the hands. Tenderness means to use our eyes to see the other, our ears to hear the other, to listen to the children, the poor, those who are afraid of the future. To listen also to the silent cry of our common home, of our sick and polluted earth. Tenderness means to use our hands and our heart to comfort the other, to take care of those in need.[12]

These words were a powerful and timely reminder that even when it seems the voices of rejection and division and fear will prevail, the voice of love and gospel pops up in unexpected places—I mean it's the pope giving a TED talk! Life emerging in unexpected places always strikes me. For example, I delight at the sight of a tuft of grass or a single flower creeping up through a tiny crack in a sea of concrete pavement. For me, that very small thing points to a very large truth: the power of life, fueled by the love and presence of an endlessly creative God, is stubborn and determined. Life and love will always, ultimately prevail. There are visions and reminders of this truth everywhere in creation.

Psalm 19 captures this wisdom: "The heavens are telling the glory of God; / and the firmament proclaims [God's] handiwork" (Ps 19:1). Poet Gerard Manley Hopkins expands upon the psalm in "God's Grandeur." It is a beautifully evocative poem, full of imagery that is at once earthly and transcendent, as in these lines:

And though the last lights off the black West went
Oh, morning, at the brown brink eastward, springs

Whenever I share a poem of any kind, I can't help thinking of my dad who loved to tell the story of his college English class in which his reaction to poetry—as an accounting major—was general frustration and aggravation. "Why not just say what you mean?" he'd ask. He may not have used any formal poetic way of speaking, but my dad did speak with the wisdom of the poets and the Psalms. In the face of my worry or stress, Daddy regularly reminded me that "the sun comes up every morning and there's nothing we can do to change that." This, just another way of saying, as Hopkins does, that for all our human smear and smudge, "nature is never spent" and "morning, at the brown brink eastward, springs" every day. From my window, I often watch the sun rise; and it proclaims something powerful: it is a new day, a new start, a new life. I can begin again. It is a regular reminder of God's love that is new every morning.

One of the things that consistently helps me regain a sense of balance, hope, and general well-being in the face of anxiety and stress is to be outside, to look at the trees, to listen to the birds, to walk barefoot on the grass, to feel the breeze against my skin, to smell the scent of flowers or wet earth. It recalibrates my blood pressure to pet and play with the dogs and cat who share our home. Even if it's with the aid of allergy medicine or a great picture window through which to take it in, my guess is that all of us can be fed and nourished by intentional engagement with earth, wind, fire, water, and all the plants and creatures and energies in this beautiful world. The animals and plants speak; they teach us things about life and about God. You never know when you will see or receive something that restores your hope, that calls you back to something more real than all the litigation and destruction so prevalent all around us. Wendell Berry gives us this vision:

> After the bitter nights
> and the gray, cold days
> comes a bright afternoon.
> I go into the creek valley
> and there are the horses, the black
> and the white, lying in the warm
> shine on a bed of dry hay.
> They lie side by side,
> identically posed as a painter
> might imagine them:
> heads up, ears and eyes
> alert. They are beautiful in the light
> and in the warmth happy. Such
> harmonies are rare. This is
> not the way the world
> is. It is a possibility
> nonetheless deeply seeded
> within the world. It is
> the way the world is sometimes.[13]

One of the ways we may find renewal on the journey is to intentionally experience the created world. You never know when you will catch a glimpse of harmony. You never know when you'll be given the gift of experiencing the way the world is sometimes. The world *is* that way sometimes; and ultimately, by God's grace and in God's mercy, it *will* be that way always, when, in the fullness of time, all things are reconciled and made new.

Receive Some Good News

Who doesn't love good news? Receiving good news is like being offered a drink of cool water on a hot day, refreshing and nourishing. But it often feels like there is an absence of much good news. Disturbing news, confusing news, and bad news is readily available and always popping up on our screens—screens that go with us everywhere. This constant stream of disturbing news can do real damage to our mental and emotional state.

Mary McNaughton-Cassill, a professor at the University of Texas at San Antonio and leading researcher on the connection between media consumption and stress, is clear that folks who suffer from mental illnesses like anxiety and depression need to be very careful about their news intake. And for all of us, taking in bad news can contribute to a sense of helplessness and "can also lead us to gradually see the world as a darker and darker place, chipping away at certain optimistic tendencies."[14]

For those of us committed to sacred resistance, we absolutely need to "stay awake" and informed. But we also have to be mindful of the effects of what we are "taking in." Just as our bodies need a balanced diet, our psyches and souls need a balanced diet as well. Feeding ourselves only bad news will make us sick.

"The light of the eyes rejoices the heart, / and good news refreshes the body" (Prov 15:30). My study Bible says that "the light of the eyes" refers to "the cheerful look of the messenger." In other words, the way the message is communicated makes a difference. And "good news refreshes the body" is pretty straightforward. We need to both monitor the intake of challenging news and feed ourselves with good news that is communicated with "light" in the eyes. How do we do this?

Jesse Singal, quoting McNaughton-Cassill, suggests that the most important way of guarding against the negative effects of the news is to "get conscious":

> That is, stop consuming news like a hungry teenager wolfs down a Pop-Tart.... "You have to get some control mentally."... The more you understand your own reaction to the news, the easier it will be to shape your news-consumption habits in an adaptive way. It's also useful to see the bigger pictures, of course. "Consciously focus yourself on the evidence around you that the news is picking out the extremes and the bad things," McNaughton-Cassill said.[15]

The invitation here is to understand that there are many reasons news and social media channels prioritize controversial and negative content, some of which are purely self-serving. In other words, bad news is not all there is to share!

So that's some guidance for how to manage our intake of challenging news. But what about balancing the diet with some good stuff? I am aware of several sources that exist to share good news—the stories that don't generally take center stage in mainstream media. A few include "The Optimist," a weekly e-newsletter from *The Washington Post*, and a couple of websites that curate stories that have the potential to "refresh the body": one called "Daily Good" and another called "Good News Network."[16] What if you replaced your computer's Internet landing page with one of these sites? What would it be like to be inundated with interesting, positive stories first, rather than the junk that so often fills our screens?

Yes, we need to stay awake and aware. Yes, there is a lot of injustice and struggle to which we need to give attention. And if we are really paying attention, we know that—even in the midst of all the challenge—in God's world there is always more than enough good news to go around. Why not partake? Why not share? Because, God knows, everyone's hungry.

Hold On to Each Other

"We hold on to each other and trust that God holds on to us." I often hear myself repeating these words to folks in moments of crisis. There is much over which we have no control, but the thing we can do is hold on to each other! We can choose whether or not to stay connected in relationship, to care for the relationships that matter most, to give and receive the support available—support that's essential—for the work of life, faith, and sacred resistance. A favorite poem from Hafiz, titled "A Great Need," captures the heart of the gift:

Out
Of a great need
We are all holding hands
And climbing.
Not loving is a letting go.
Listen,
The terrain around here
Is
Far too
Dangerous
For
That.[17]

Holding on to one another is what we can do. We can try to love one another. In times of crisis and stress, when "the terrain is...dangerous," it can be tempting to forget how important it is to attend to the relationships around us. Over the past months, I've heard about how folks are trying to cope with living their already-full lives with the added stress, outrage, fear, and uncertainty that has gotten stirred by the presidential campaign, election, and subsequent events. A common concern is the toll these things were taking on relationships. This has been loudest with regard to family members who hold opposing political views. But I also have heard—spoken almost in a whisper—that marriages are feeling the effects, that the stresses are finding their way into folks' closest relationships. It should come as no surprise that this is the case. All our "stuff" shows up in our primary relationships in one way or another, for better or for worse.

The rather dark and cranky wisdom of Qoheleth in the book of Ecclesiastes suggests this about relationships: "Two are better than one...for if they fall, one will lift up the other; but woe to one who is alone and falls and does not have another to help. Again, if two lie together, they keep warm; but how can one keep warm alone?" (Eccl 4:9-11). In other words, we need one another. Trying to "go it alone" is a pretty daunting task and, even if we can persevere for a while, there will come a time when we just can't do what we need to do without the help of another person. We are created to be in relationship and, regardless of the shape, size, or makeup of our family and circle of friends, the primary relationships in our lives are a profound source of sustenance. Sometimes we let other things in our lives—work, bad habits, or emotional baggage—get in the way of nurturing and fully receiving the gifts of those relationships.

Over the years, I have known many folks who found their marriage in shambles from years of failure to communicate; I have witnessed children alienated from their parents due to lack of time spent together; I have watched friendships sour through failure to show up for one another. My focus here, however, is not on broken relationships—or on tragic instances of abuse, betrayal, and the like. Rather, it is a simple reminder that there is nothing more important than the primary relationships we have in our lives, that these relationships deserve our care and attention, and that they are a source of deep nourishment.

Any meaningful relationship will require care, cultivation, patience, and work. Like a garden, our relationships need to be lovingly tended or they can become dry, unmanageable, even unrecognizable. Healthy relationships require an investment of time. In my own life, I do OK with some relationships, less OK with others. And always, I can do better. Recently, I noticed clergy colleagues posting on social media about their struggles to be a good friend—about how ministry in the church always seems to override making time for friendships. I can relate! Our work responsibilities—no matter what they are—can become so all-consuming that we have little time or energy for friends or anyone else. My further challenge is that even when I have held aside time to spend with my spouse, he often gets the worst of me since I have been so intent on trying to give my best to everyone else. Perhaps you understand what I'm talking about. We can be patient, open, creative, engaged with others, but when it comes to our partner, parent, or child?

When we are sad, tired, angry, afraid, it might be tempting to "let go" of the hand of your loved ones—through isolation, aggression, taking out frustration on them, and so on. It can be tempting, when we feel the weight of responsibility upon us, to take those closest to us for granted. But what a gift it is when we are in a difficult place and have a friend who holds on to us, assuring us we're not alone. What a gift when we are able to lean upon the love of a partner or spouse. What a gift when time spent with our children reminds us of what matters most of all. What a gift when a beloved companion helps us remember to laugh and to play and to trust God.

Sacred resistance is a steep climb and a long journey. Remember to care for those closest to you on the way. Hold on to each other and trust that God holds on to you.

Find Your Strength in Quietness and Trust

Thus said the Lord GOD, the Holy One of Israel: In returning and rest you shall be saved; in quietness and in trust shall be your strength. (Isa 30:15a)

To trust and rest in God is an orientation of the heart, mind, and soul that keeps us humble and open. If we stay close to God, we will be mindful of our dependence and smallness. This is not to suggest that we are insignificant. It's to suggest that you are not God (nor am I!). Choosing to turn to God keeps us from being blinded by the perverse notion that the world revolves around us. And that allows us to remember that our perspective is not the only one, that we always have more to learn. And we're at least occasionally aware that we are part of a reality much larger than us. Returning to God saves us from a small, self-obsessed life and from trying to save ourselves, others, or the world on our own.

Resting in God keeps us close to the things that matter most of all: compassion, kindness, justice, gentleness, friendship, joy, wonder, and solidarity. In other words, nearness to God helps us separate the wheat from the chaff—the nourishing from the junk food—as we move through our days. It saves us from getting distracted by things that don't matter. Over the past months, when I felt most vulnerable to getting sucked into the desolating news cycles and foolishness, I found these words from Philippians floating to the surface during my prayer: "whatever is true, whatever is honorable, whatever is just, whatever is pure, whatever is pleasing, whatever is commendable, if there is any excellence and if there is anything worthy of praise, think about these things" (Phil 4:8).

Abiding in God keeps us close to God's love for us, for others, and for the creation. Trusting God's eternal, steadfast love allows us to live every moment more fully—not shrinking back in fear of failure or judgment or even death. It allows us to say, "God loves me and is for me. So whatever you've got: Bring. It. On."

Returning to God and trusting in God strengthens us to live with purpose and power and saves us from the soul-killing idolatries that always tempt us. But there are times when I am startled to realize that as much as I may know these things in my head, the message has still not fully taken up residence in my heart. What are the disappointing signals that this is so? Restlessness and agitation—what we call "overfunctioning" these days—and visceral anxiety that I'm going to fail are among my red flags. I imagine you can identify your own.

Five years ago during my annual seven-day silent retreat, I was struggling to be quiet and still, to get my mind to stop spinning, to release all the needs and work responsibilities that were weighing me down with worry. The prompt from my spiritual director was to prayerfully put myself into Matthew 8:23-27, the story of Jesus asleep on a boat with his disciples when a storm erupts. The invitation was to be on the boat, to see Jesus asleep, and to ask myself, "What do I want to say or do to him?" I reacted to the first line of the story, "When [Jesus] got into the boat, his disciples followed him" (Matt 8:23). I found myself thinking, "You got me into this, Jesus! I wouldn't be in this boat in the middle of a storm if you hadn't led me here!" My gut reaction was to be angry at Jesus, to blame and accuse Jesus: "You don't even care!"

Then I became aware of the strong winds (being from Oklahoma, strong winds scare me. Hello tornadoes!); and then I remembered that I don't know anything about boats; and then I thought of how vulnerable human bodies are in the middle of the sea. As I stayed in the boat with all these thoughts and feelings, I looked again at Jesus just lying there sleeping, and I realized that what I really wanted to know was: how is Jesus sleeping under these conditions? And then I realized my real question was: how can *I* do that? And the word I received then was an invitation: "Just as you followed me into the boat, follow me into my rest."

What does it mean to follow Jesus into his rest? The thing is that we know how to follow into the boat, to be engaged in all the activity and the planning and the study and the work and the organizing and the advocacy and the writing and sacred resistance. We know how to follow Jesus onto the boat; you may even know how to row the boat, how to care for the people on the boat, how to chart a course, and so on. But when things get hairy and scary, do we know how to follow Jesus into his rest? In *rest* is salvation.

Jesus slept even when the storm raged. Jesus shows us how to be still, to be at peace, in the midst of the things swirling around us that tempt us to panic. This does not mean that we crawl under a blanket and hide from or fail to respond to the challenges of the world. Rather, the story reveals that even in the middle of danger, we can rest in God, we can look to Christ who is a steady, still, trustworthy presence who has *got us*, who is holding us in love.

We can intellectually understand that from reading the story. But we only learn to really *know and trust* in the presence of God by actually spending time in the presence of God. We learn how to bring ourselves to rest in God's presence by practicing silence and stillness, by being intentionally aware of God's presence and by listening for God's voice. Following Jesus into his rest trains your senses to be able—even right in the middle of the scary, stormy realities of your life and of our world—to hear Jesus say to *you*, "Peace, be still." And to know that Christ has the power to make it so. "In returning and rest you shall be saved; / in quietness and in trust shall be your strength."

Years ago, one of my mentors "assigned" me a prayer: "God, help me trust you more than I distrust myself." My mentor knew me well. Over the years, I've added to the prayer a bit: "Help me trust you, God, more than I distrust myself or anyone or anything else. Just help me trust you." That trust in God's presence, in God's love, in God's steadfast desire to grant mercy and grace, is powerful. It sets us free to risk making a choice, to risk taking a step, to risk making a mistake. In quietness and trust we learn that God will never leave us to face the perils of this world alone. And that means every one of us can face the perils of this world as citizens of the Kin-dom, as agents of sacred resistance—with love, with wisdom, and with courage.

NOTES

Preface

1. Ginger E. Gaines-Cirelli, "Testify!" Foundry United Methodist Church, November 13, 2016, http://www.foundryumc.org/sermons/testify.

2. At Foundry, we often use the word *kin-dom* in place of *kingdom* to reflect a gender-neutral view of God's community, the "kinship" we share with all humanity, and the belief that God's vision for creation is about loving, mutual relationship.

3. Fred Kaan, "For the Healing of the Nations," *United Methodist Hymnal* (Nashville: The United Methodist Publishing House, 1989), 428.

Introduction

1. Michael Walzer, "The Politics of Resistance," *Dissent Magazine*, March 1, 2017, https://www.dissentmagazine.org/online_articles/the-politics-of-resistance-michael-walzer.

2. Ibid.

3. Theologian Douglas John Hall describes the Christian understanding of "being" as "something we are always being *given*, like... 'daily bread'...our being-with God, our own kind, and otherkind. Being, in the tradition of Jerusalem...is 'with-being' (*Mitsein*)." He goes on to say that "salvation means beginning to be with these others: a

coexistence which is at the same time pro-existence" (*The Confessing Church* [Minneapolis: Fortress Press, 1996], 43).

4. Maya Angelou, "On the Pulse of Morning," *Maya Angelou: The Complete Poetry* (New York: Random House, 2015), 266.

1. Sacred Resistance: Contours and Commitments

1. Douglas John Hall, *The Confessing Church* (Minneapolis: Fortress Press, 1996), 12.

2. Ibid., 393.

2. Caring for the Good of All

1. Eric H. F. Law, "Mutual Invitation as Mutual Empowerment," *The Wolf Shall Dwell with the Lamb: A Spirituality for Leadership in a Multicultural Community* (St. Louis: Chalice Press, 1993), 79–88.

2. A microaggression is indirect, subtle, or unintentional discrimination against members of a marginalized group.

3. Kimberlé Crenshaw, "Demarginalizing the Intersection of Race and Sex: A Black Feminist Critique of Antidiscrimination Doctrine, Feminist Theory and Antiracist Politics," 1989, https://philpapers.org/archive/CREDTI.pdf.

4. Ibid.

5. Ibid.

6. Catholic News Service, https://cruxnow.com/cns/2016/09/03/big-fruits-mother-teresas-small-things-love/.

7. Southern Poverty Law Center, https://www.splcenter.org/fighting-hate/extremist-files/individual/richard-bertrand-spencer-0.

8. Chris Newman (@sylvanaqua), "A Message to Charlottesville about Lee Park from Your Local Black Farmer," Facebook, May 17, 2017, https://www.facebook.com/sylvanaqua/photos/a.332916656839641.1073741829.332425060222134/1036321936499106/?type=3&theater.

9. Walter Wink, "Beyond Just War and Pacifism: Jesus' Nonviolent Way," http://www.cres.org/star/_wink.htm.

10. Ginger E. Gaines-Cirelli, "Security at What Cost?" (adapted),

Foundry United Methodist Church, March 12, 2017, http://www
.foundryumc.org/sermons/security-what-cost.

11. For example, "Nonviolence and Racial Justice," *A Testament of
Hope: The Essential Writings and Speeches of Martin Luther King, Jr.*, ed.
James M. Washington (New York: HarperOne, 1986), 7–8.

12. Ibid., 8.

13. Curtiss Paul DeYoung, "From Resistance to Reconciliation,"
Resist! Christian Dissent for the 21st Century, ed. Michael G. Long (New
York: Orbis Books, 2008), 15.

14. See the Northumbria Community, *Celtic Daily Prayer: Book
Two, Farther Up and Farther In* (London: William Collins, 2015), 1088.

3. Sacred Resistance: A Way of Life for the Church

1. Douglas John Hall, *The Confessing Church* (Minneapolis: Fortress
Press, 1996), 335.

2. Ibid., 336.

3. Stanley Hauerwas and William H. Willimon, *Resident Aliens:
Life in the Christian Colony*, expanded ed. (Nashville: Abingdon Press,
2014), 46–47.

4. Walter Brueggemann, *The Prophetic Imagination*, 2nd ed. (Minneapolis: Fortress Press, 2001), 117–18.

5. What I am addressing here is the tendency to "de-mythologize"
the Christian faith or to cut off the dependence on God's active participation with us (either consciously or unconsciously), leaving the burden
of "saving the world" on the shoulders of human enterprise. It seems
to me that many self-defined "progressives" tend toward this error; the
"progress" seems to depend on social systems and better human solutions
without reference to the fact that God is really present and involved.

6. Letty Russell, *Church in the Round: Feminist Interpretation of the
Church* (Louisville, KY: Westminster John Knox Press, 1993), 115.

7. Stanley Hauerwas and William H. Willimon, *Resident Aliens:
Life in the Christian Colony*, expanded ed. (Nashville: Abingdon Press,
2014), 47.

8. Ginger E. Gaines-Cirelli, "What It Takes" (adapted), Foundry
United Methodist Church, March 25, 2016, http://www.foundryumc
.org/sermons/what-it-takes.

4. Prophetic Guidance for the Living of These Days

1. Much of this chapter previously appeared in *Prophecy: A Foundation for Sacred Resistance*, published by Foundry United Methodist Church in 2017, available at http://www.foundryumc.org/prophecy.

2. Walter Brueggemann, *The Prophetic Imagination*, 2nd ed. (Minneapolis: Fortress Press, 2001), 3.

3. Ibid.

4. Ibid., xvii.

5. Ibid.

6. Ibid., xvi.

7. Ibid.

8. Ibid.

9. Ibid., 13–15.

10. Ibid., 81.

11. Ibid., 35.

12. Ibid., 91.

13. Ibid., 40.

14. Ibid., 65.

15. Ibid., 40.

16. Wendell Berry, "Manifesto: The Mad Farmer Liberation Front" from *The Country of Marriage* (San Diego: Harcourt Brace Jovanovich, 1973).

17. Brueggemann, *Prophetic Imagination*, 13–15.

18. Ibid., 60.

19. Ibid.

20. Joan Chittister, *Joan Chittister: Essential Writings* (New York: Orbis, 2014), 164.

21. Harry Emerson Fosdick, "God of Grace and God of Glory," in *The United Methodist Hymnal* (Nashville: The United Methodist Publishing House, 1989), 577.

5. Stop Speaking "Smooth" Things

1. Michael Gerson, "An Administration without a Conscience," Opinions, *The Washington Post*, July 13, 2017, https://www.washingtonpost.com/opinions/in-trumps-world-innocence-is-proved

-by-guilt/2017/07/13/07e69a82-67ea-11e7-8eb5-cbccc2e7bfbf_story
.html.

2. David Walsh, *Selling Out America's Children: How America Puts Profits before Values and What Parents Can Do* (Minneapolis: Fairview Press, 1996).

3. Wendell Berry, *This Day: Sabbath Poems Collected and New 1979–2013* (Berkeley: Counterpoint, 2013), 350.

4. Rev. Dr. Otis Moss III, "The Blue Note Gospel: Preaching the Prophetic Blues in a Post-Soul World" (Lyman Beecher Lectures, Yale Divinity School, New Haven, CT, 2014).

5. Wendell Berry, "1991: I," *This Day: Sabbath Poems Collected and New 1979–2013* (Berkeley: Counterpoint, 2013), 105.

6. Walter Brueggemann, "Voices of the Night—against Justice," in *To Act Justly, Love Tenderly, Walk Humbly*, ed. Walter Brueggemann, Sharon Parks, and Thomas H. Groome (Mahwah, NJ: Paulist Press, 1986), 5.

7. Martin Luther King Jr., "Letter from Birmingham City Jail," *A Testament of Hope: The Essential Writings and Speeches of Martin Luther King, Jr.*, ed. James M. Washington (New York: HarperOne, 1986), 291.

8. William Sloane Coffin, *Credo* (Louisville: Westminster John Knox Press, 2004), 67.

6. What Do We Do?

1. Jonathan Wilson-Hartgrove, *New Monasticism: What It Has to Say to Today's Church* (Grand Rapids: Brazos Press, 2008), 11.

2. Ibid., 9.

3. Ibid., 10.

4. See Bonaro W. Overstreet, "Stubborn Ounces," *Signature: New and Selected Poems* (New York: Norton & Co., Inc., 1978), 19.

5. Douglas John Hall, *The Confessing Church* (Minneapolis: Fortress Press, 1996), 133.

6. David McRaney, "Confirmation Bias," You Are Not So Smart, June 23, 2010, https://youarenotsosmart.com/2010/06/23/confirmation-bias/.

7. Ibid.

8. Ibid.

9. Ginger E. Gaines-Cirelli, "We Welcome" (adapted), Foundry

United Methodist Church, October 16, 2016, http://www.foundry umc.org/sermons/we-welcome.../.

10. Dawna Markova, "I Will Not Die an Unlived Life," Awakin, February 11, 2008, http://www.awakin.org/read/view.php?tid=552.

11. Hall, *The Confessing Church*, 343–404.

12. Ibid., 373.

13. Ibid.

14. Ibid., 379.

15. Ibid., 378.

16. Tom Berlin, "Preaching to the Polarized," *Circuit Rider*, Aug/Sept /Oct 2016, http://www.ministrymatters.com/all/entry/7560/preaching -to-the-polarized.

17. Ibid.

18. Hall, *The Confessing Church*, 395.

19. Ginger E. Gaines-Cirelli, "Choosing Sides" (adapted), Foundry United Methodist Church, November 20. 2016, http://www .foundryumc.org/sermons/choosing-sides.

7. Fueling the Resistance: Guarding against Burnout

1. Much of the material in this chapter is adapted from a sermon series I preached from April 23, 2017, through May 28, 2017, called "Soul Food." You can find those sermons on Foundry United Methodist Church's website at http://www.foundryumc.org/previous-sermons.

2. Debbie McGauran, "The 6 Health Benefits of Laughter," Activebeat, October 14, 2017, http://www.activebeat.com/your-health /the-6-health-benefits-of-laughter/5/.

3. Lawrence Robinson, Melinda Smith, and Jeanne Segal, "Laughter Is the Best Medicine," Helpguide.org, October 2017, https://www .helpguide.org/articles/emotional-health/laughter-is-the-best-medicine .htm.

4. McGauran, "The 6 Health Benefits of Laughter."

5. Anne Lamott, "Anne Lamott: The Habit of Practice," Faith & Leadership, July 4, 2011, https://www.faithandleadership.com/anne -lamott-habit-practice.

6. Ibid.

7. Carolyn Arends, "Carbonated Holiness: Laughter Is Serious

Business," Renovaré, January 20, 2017, https://renovare.org/articles/carbonated-holiness.

8. See Robinson, Smith, and Segal, "Laughter Is the Best Medicine."

9. Ibid.

10. Arends, "Carbonated Holiness."

11. Pope Francis, "Why the Only Future Worth Building Includes Everyone," TED, April 2017, https://www.ted.com/talks/pope_francis_why_the_only_future_worth_building_includes_everyone/transcript.

12. Ibid.

13. Wendell Berry, "2008: I," in *This Day: Collected & New Sabbath Poems* (Berkeley: Counterpoint, 2013), 315.

14. Jesse Singal, "What All This Bad News Is Doing to Us," *New York Magazine*, August 8, 2014, http://nymag.com/scienceofus/2014/08/what-all-this-bad-news-is-doing-to-us.html.

15. Ibid.

16. See https://subscribe.washingtonpost.com/newsletters/#/newsletters (look for "The Optimist" and "Inspired Life"), http://www.dailygood.org/, and http://www.goodnewsnetwork.org/.

17. Hafiz, "A Great Need," in *The Gift*, trans. Daniel Ladinsky (New York: Penguin Compass, 1999), 165.